After Kafka

After Kafka

The Influence of Kafka's Fiction

Shimon Sandbank

The University of Georgia Press

Athens and London

© 1989 by the University of Georgia Press
Athens, Georgia 30602
All rights reserved
Designed by Mary Mendell
Set in Galliard
The paper in this book meets the guidelines for
permanence and durability of the Committee on
Production Guidelines for Book Longevity of the
Council on Library Resources.
Printed in the United States of America
93 92 91 90 89   5 4 3 2 1

Library of Congress Cataloging in Publication Data

Sandbank, Shimon.
    After Kafka : the influence of Kafka's fiction / Shimon
    Sandbank.
        p. cm.
    Bibliography: p.
    Includes index.
    ISBN 0-8203-1105-7 (alk. paper)
        1. Fiction—20th century—History and criticism.
        2. Kafka, Franz, 1883–1924—Influence. I. Title.
PN3503.S28 1989
809'.04—dc19   88-24995
                                            CIP

British Library Cataloging in Publication Data available

For Tirza

Contents

Acknowledgments

Earlier versions of two chapters of this book have been previously published as separate journal articles. I am grateful to the editors for permission to reprint them: "Effing the Ineffable: Beckett and Kafka" (an early version of chapter 5), in *Hebrew University Studies in Literature and the Arts,* vol. 12, no. 2 (Autumn 1984); and "Parable and Theme: Kafka and American Fiction" (an early version of chapter 10), in *Comparative Literature,* vol. 37, no. 3 (Summer 1985).

I wish to thank those of my students in the Department of Comparative Literature of the Hebrew University, Jerusalem, whose honest queries surprised me into rethinking some truisms I had been taking for granted.

I also wish to thank my university for various grants and particularly for granting me a sabbatical during the academic year 1983–84, which made it possible to complete this book.

I am grateful to Mrs. Sylvia Farhi, excellent typist and a joy to work with.

I am above all indebted to three colleagues and friends: Ruth Ginsburg, Baruch Hochman, and Shlomith Rimmon-Kenan. All three, each from his very different vantage point, tactfully exposed my incoherencies and generously added their own insights.

Truth and Transmissibility

Kafka's real genius was that he tried something entirely new: he sacrificed truth for the sake of clinging to its transmissibility, its aggadic element.
—*Walter Benjamin, letter to Gershom Scholem*

I   In an essay written on the tenth anniversary of Kafka's death, Walter Benjamin speaks of his stories as "gestic theater," "a code of gestures," so many "acts in the 'Nature Theater of Oklahoma.'" These gestures, he says, "had no definite symbolic meaning for the author from the outset." Instead, "he divests the human gesture of its traditional supports and then has a subject for reflection without end."[1]

The same profound insight is then put into other terms: Jewish *Aggadah* versus *Halakhah*. These two terms call for some explanation. They refer to two categories of Jewish rabbinic teaching, usually defined in contradistinction to each other: *Halakhah* as those parts of the Talmud concerned with religious laws and regulations, and *Aggadah* as those sections of the Talmud and Midrash containing "homiletic expositions of the Bible, stories, legends, folklore, anecdotes or maxims."[2] *Aggadah,* with its predominantly narrative character, is not regarded "as authoritative in the same normative way as the *Halakhah* is obligatory," and Maimonides even says it is "comparable to metaphors of poems."[3]

To Benjamin, Kafka's parables have "a similar relationship to doctrine as the *Aggadah* does to the *Halakhah*. They are not parables, and yet they do not want to be taken at their face value; they lend themselves to quotations and can be told for purposes of clarification. But do we have the doctrine which Kafka's parables interpret and which K.'s postures and the gestures of his animals clarify? It does not exist; all we can say is that here and there we have an allusion to it. Kafka might have said that these are relics transmitting the doctrine, although we could regard them just as well as precursors preparing the doctrine."[4]

Gestic theater without symbolic meaning and interpretative *Aggadah* without a *Halakhah* to interpret: both metaphors point to what was startlingly new in Kafka. The juxtaposition of elaborate gesture and inaccessible meaning, of minute detail and unknowable whole is the most striking feature of his way of writing: Samsa's metamorphosed body and movement versus the inexplicable metamorphosis itself; or Joseph K.'s wanderings in offices and corridors versus the incomprehensible guilt itself. If movement and gesture were presented as semantically self-sufficient, or, obversely, were their symbolic meaning determinable, there would be nothing new about this way of writing. What makes it entirely new is that it always points to a truth beyond itself but never commits itself to the truth to which it points.

Benjamin's essay thus suggests a radically new concept in Kafka of the very status of fiction. His stories present themselves as interpretations, point to a text beyond them, but are deprived of the doctrine they interpret. They become vehicles without tenor, a secret code whose secret is irrecoverable. Their message being lost—or, as Benjamin suggests, still in the making—they can yield no theme, no idea relatable to the real world.[5] They are inherently open-ended, fragmentary, and truncated. They are so many pointers to an unknown meaning.

To relate this to some prevalent distinctions[6] one could perhaps speak of a threefold gap at the center of Kafka's stories: at the level of the events as they appear in the text (what the Russian formalists call the *sjužet*), at the level of the events in their original "natural" order, before they were artistically shaped into the text, or after being abstracted from it (what formalists call the *fabula*), and, most important, at the level of the theme. A temporary gap at the level of the *sjužet* is finally filled in, after many arrests and retardations. But the filling proves illusory and the gap is reasserted and finalized. It now turns out to be at the level of the *fabula* itself, a permanent gap. The absurd nature of the gap, as well as of the story as a whole, makes the reader treat the story as symbolic, makes him want to translate it into another mode. The various clues scattered in the text suggest several possibilities for such translation, but none "seems to encompass everything notable in the semantic universe,"[7] and each, moreover, is contradicted by some elements in the text. Thus, "we cannot discover a level at which interpretation may rest."[8] The text's enigmatic face requires translation but it defies any accepted doctrine—Christianity, Marxism, psychoanalysis— that would make consistent translation possible. While the gaps at the level of the *sjužet* and the *fabula* are by no means peculiar to Kafka and can exist, of course, without the gap at the level of the theme, it is this latter gap that is the *differentia specifica* of Kafka's type of fiction.

To make this clearer let me use the example of *The Castle*. The obvious, though not only, gap at the level of the *sjužet* is How can one get to the Castle? K.'s many attempts to answer this question constitute the bulk of the novel. Then, toward the end, the secretary Bürgel answers it when he tells K., in chapter 18, that what he ought to do is to surprise an incompetent secretary in the middle of the night. For several reasons to be pointed out later on, this answer is a nonanswer and the gap is finalized and turns out to be at the level of the *fabula* itself. The way to the Castle remains undisclosed, at least to the dominant consciousness, that of K. But the story of a man incapable of getting to a place within a stone's throw from where he is, is too absurd not to require a symbolic interpretation. We are thus pressed by elements in the text to translate the incidents in terms of our favorite disciplines, concerns, or systems of thought. The inaccessibility of the Castle to K., for example, is translated into the inaccessibility of grace to Everyman, or of the state authorities to the Jew, or of incestuous sex objects to the infant, and so on. Each translation, however, while suggested by certain elements in the text, is contradicted by others. None encompasses everything in the semantic universe of the novel. No thematic extrapolation seems satisfactory. Thus, the crucial gap turns out to exist at the level of the theme itself. The fictive world is divorced from any final meaning in the real world.

At the same time, to present Kafka as a purely self-reflexive writer would be to ignore the obvious metaphysical thrust of his work. The strategy I have described is complicated by the fact that, with all its refusal to commit itself to a theme, Kafka's work is guided by an undeniable metaphysical impulse. Although its truth is "lost," although the themes it evokes—and evades—may be psychological or political no less than metaphysical, its very resistance to a reduction to any one of them is a measure of its holistic, metaphysical drive. Were it not for the fact that the doctrine Kafka was after was the total meaning of existence, the total truth of ontology rather than the partial truths of psychology or ethics or politics, he could have had a doctrine, not only its "relics." The fact that Kafka's stories resist thematic extrapolation is inseparable from the fact that they are metaphysical and concerned with the world as a totality.

Kafka's characters want to see the world as a totality, but this is impossible. Already the Supplicant in Kafka's earliest story, "Description of a Struggle," longs to see things "as they are before they show themselves to him"[9]—to jump out of his consciousness and overcome the partiality of his perspective. But this, as Kafka writes in his diary, is impossible: "Immediate contact with the workaday world deprives me—though inwardly I am as detached as I can be—of the possibility of taking a broad view of matters, just as if I were at the bottom of a ravine, with my head bowed down in addition" (*D* 326).[10] Insisting on taking the broadest view of matters while being aware of its inherent impossibility, and yet opting for literature instead of silence, Kafka, like the king's couriers in one of his aphorisms, must post through the world shouting senseless messages.

As suggested, however, Kafka's novels do contain, toward their ends, a scene in which the gap seems to be filled out and a doctrine found at last. I am referring to the "Nature Theater of Oklahoma" in *America,* the cathedral scene in *The Trial,* and the above-mentioned Bürgel scene in *The Castle.* The first two have the obvious trappings of revelation and a revealed way to salvation. In *America* angels and trumpets and supper in Heaven accompany Karl Rossmann's feeling of being finally accepted. In *The Trial* space and darkness and the priest's roaring voice lead up to what seems like a holy text, the parable "Before the Law" and its interpreted message. The Bürgel scene is definitely less sublime, but there too an offer is made "to settle the whole affair up there in no time at all" (*C* 316). Bürgel seems to tell K. at last how to get to the Castle.

But do these three scenes disprove Benjamin's claim that there is no doctrine in Kafka? Do they make thematic extrapolation possible, thus restoring the novels to the status of decodable codes, perhaps even of a Bildungsroman? They do not. It is arguable, indeed, that they exist merely to underline the absence of any final message. They do so in different ways. In the "Nature Theater of Oklahoma" it is the ambiguity of symbols and verbal formulas—angelic and satanic, religious and sacriligious, real and made of papier-mâché—that creates an unresolvable tension and cancels out the message of acceptance in the very process of stating it. In *The Trial*, the text interpreted—the parable "Before the Law"—is ransacked, in the "exegesis" that follows it, for all contradictory meanings, thus becoming a *mise-en-abyme* of the entire novel, perhaps of Kafka's entire oeuvre, a glaring case of *Aggadah* without *Halakhah*. The conclusions drawn from the parable cancel each other out. "So the door-keeper deluded the man," "so you think the man was not deluded," "the deluded person is really the door-keeper" follow each other (*T* 237–40), all mere expressions of the "commentator's despair"[11] vis-à-vis the "unalterable" text (*T* 240). The text itself, or rather the law it propounds, is finally said to be "set beyond human judgement." So are the words of the doorkeeper who belongs to the law. "It is not necessary to accept everything as true, one must only accept it as necessary" is the priest's final caveat (*T* 243), rejecting all human understanding and ipso facto any understandable message.

Joseph K.'s response, "A melancholy conclusion. It turns lying into a universal principle," is "not his final judgement" (*T* 243). He must somehow feel that his judgment is wrong, that he has misunderstood the priest's words. It is necessity, not lying, that the priest opposes to truth. A nihilistic conclusion like Joseph K.'s is as false as any other, for it equally applies human judgment to the law, to the ultimate meaning of things. The law is neither truth nor falsehood:

it is the necessity of given facts. Misunderstanding this postulate, Joseph K. finds he is too tired to follow such "unfamiliar" trains of thought. No wonder, for he is asked no more and no less than to give up reason.

Perhaps a reference to a deconstructive treatment of the same parable may throw further light on this point. Jacques Derrida discussed "Before the Law" in a lecture read to the Royal Institute of Philosophy in 1982 and later included, in its original French version, in the institute's lecture series.[12] If Benjamin speaks of *Aggadah* that has lost the *Halakhah* behind it, implying that they once coexisted, Derrida here claims that law (*loi*) and story (*récit*) *must* exclude each other by definition. The categorical authority of the law requires it to be without history or any derivation that would relativize it. If one insists on telling stories about the law, they must be limited to circumstances, events external to the law, or, at the most, modes of its revelation.

The man from the country in Kafka's parable is, to Derrida, the story that tries to approach the law, enter into relations with it, enter it and become intrinsic to it—but "none of these can succeed." The very essence of the law is that it reveals itself by hiding, without saying where it came from or where it is: "Ce qui reste invisible et caché en chaque loi, on peut donc supposer que c'est la loi elle-même."

Next, an analogy is drawn between the inaccessible law and the inaccessible final meaning of a story, its "unreadability" in Derrida's parlance: "Ce qui nous tient en arrêt devant la loi, comme l'homme de la campagne, n'est-ce pas aussi ce qui nous paralyse et nous retient devant un récit? . . . D'une certaine manière, *Vor dem Gesetz* est le récit de cette inaccessibilité, de cette inaccessibilité au récit, l'histoire de cette histoire impossible, la carte de ce trajet interdit." Thus, "Before the Law" becomes an allegory of "unreadability": it is a story of the way all stories must, according to the deconstructive creed, evade all definite meaning and question their own philosophical claims through their rhetoric.

Toward the end of his lecture Derrida presents another allegorical level when the man from the country, in addition to being the reader vis-à-vis the unreadable text, becomes the text itself vis-à-vis the "law" or concept of literariness that must always remain obscure: "Le texte de Kafka dit peut-être, aussi, l'être-devant-la loi de tout texte" (p. 187).

What I find rather striking about this deconstructive lecture is its totally nondeconstructive strategy. By turning Kafka's text into a twofold allegory of "unreadability"—the text's unreadability to the reader, literature's unreadability to the text—Derrida makes it very readable indeed. Its presumable message of deconstruction does not apply to itself. It is not at all treated as inaccessible or unreadable, but as brilliantly yielding two or three meanings that coexist peacefully and do not at all subvert one another. Rather than being deconstructed, Kafka's parable is reconstructed as a deconstructionist manifesto.

To find a true deconstruction of "Before the Law," one must look, as we have seen, to Kafka's own text. It is Kafka's priest who does it. Thus, Kafka serves here as a true deconstructor of his text. Derrida makes a point of discussing "Before the Law" as a separate and autonomous text—and so in fact did it appear, in Kafka's own lifetime, among the *Country Doctor* stories. But in the context of the novel it becomes the object of the fascinating process of deconstruction I have described.

The priest's words, "The Scriptures are unalterable and the comments often enough merely express the commentator's despair," could indeed serve as a splendid motto for deconstruction itself. Texts are unalterable, and our interpretations often enough merely express our despair vis-à-vis this fact. If nevertheless Kafka is not a favorite object with Derrida, and if Derrida's treatment of Kafka is not at all deconstructive, this is, paradoxically, because Kafka disarms deconstruction by being his own deconstructor.

But he is his own deconstructor in a different sense from that current among deconstructionists. The latter show "how [a discourse] undermines the philosophy it asserts, or the hierarchical oppositions on which it relies, by identifying in the text the rhetorical operations that produce the supposed ground of argument, the key concept or premise."[13] A Kafka text, on the other hand, neither asserts a philosophy nor necessitates an identification of the rhetorical operations that would question it. The questioning instead is openly thematized, incorporated into the plot itself, thus making all definitive assertion of philosophy impossible. Deconstruction, that is, is built into the text itself, not the result of an examination of the hidden implications of its rhetoric. It is plot excluding theme, not language subverting thought.

Thus, Kafka (as well as self-reflexive writers such as Borges or Robbe-Grillet) becomes a problem for deconstruction. He both embodies its strategies and disrupts its conclusions. For, on one hand, his is a shining example of a discourse that rejects all final interpretation. But, on the other hand, by doing the job of deconstruction himself, his presence and voice cannot be said to be irrelevant. It is not the free play of language that disrupts his meanings, but his own explicit skepticism.

II   But we must return from this digression to our third pseudorevelatory scene, the Bürgel episode from *The Castle*. This is the most elaborate example of a self-canceling (or, if you wish, self-deconstructing) message in Kafka. On the face of it, the secretary Bürgel is at last revealing to K. how to get to the Castle: he must surprise an incompetent secretary in the middle of the night. But this much-coveted message may be said to be deconstructed on four different levels.

First, Bürgel's speech consists of a long series of contradictions, constantly oscillating between an affirmation of the possibility of exploiting the secretaries' "nocturnal weakness" and its negation. This protracted zigag[14] ends in a number of violent paradoxes, yoking together possibility and impossibility, making redemption the cause of its own destruction: "There are, of course, opportunities that are, in a manner of speaking, too great to be made use of, there are things that are wrecked on nothing but themselves" (*C* 255).

Second, the way to the Castle, as suggested by Bürgel, is unofficial and underhand, both in that the secretary concerned is unqualified to deal with the case, and in that he is approached out of his reception hours. There is no chance of getting to the Castle openly and directly. One must come unannounced, surprise the wrong official, and exploit his "nocturnal weakness." In this sense Bürgel's entire message of redemption is put in brackets, as it were. It is a second best, whereas the open and official way is excluded a priori.

Third, while Bürgel is making his speech, K. is sinking deeper and deeper in sleep. He thus misses the message of redemption. Sleep here, as in Joseph K.'s tired response to the priest and as in many other places in Kafka, stands for the inadequacy of the mind when confronted with that which transcends it. "One's physical energies," says Bürgel, "last only to a certain limit. Who can help the fact that precisely this limit is significant in other ways too?" (*C* 254). Physical energies include, I suppose, one's mental capacity, which, ironically, ends precisely where redemption begins. Bürgel's message is once again put in brackets: it is placed outside consciousness.

Kafka's fourth and last way of deconstructing Bürgel's message is by making it a mere mirror image of what is going on while the message is being given. For Bürgel suggests that the applicant should surprise an incompetent secretary in the middle of the night, which is precisely what K. has just done: he has surprised an incompetent secretary in the middle of the night. The strict parallelism between Bürgel's message and the actual situation is strongly underlined. Bürgel, for instance, is first entirely hidden under the quilt, then talks about the scared secretary hiding under a quilt; or he talks about the applicant's irresistible fatigue while K. has actually succumbed to sleep. All that his guidance amounts to is thus simply pointing to what is happening: there it is.

It is this last point—the message as a mirror image of the random present—that most richly enacts the peculiar status of Kafka's fiction, the way it both pulls toward, and recoils from, meaning. On one hand, Bürgel's message is that the way to the Castle is any given moment, that salvation is inherent in any random act of living. On the other hand, salvation thus presented loses its very sense: for if salvation means a deliverance from state X and a transition to state Y, it must lose all sense once state X is simply equated with state Y. Bürgel's message is both the most seductive tidings of ubiquitous redemption and a message that there is no message.

III In several very short texts written in Kafka's last years, the divorce between *Aggadah* and *Halakhah,* parable and theme, becomes explicit. In the aphorism referred to above, one of the series Brod entitled "Reflections on Sin, Pain, Hope, and the True Way," the king's couriers are said to post through the world and shout to each other their messages, entirely senseless because there are no kings.[15] In "On Parables," a short text from 1922–23, the figurative nature of literary texts is taken for granted: "When the sage says: 'Go over,' he does not mean that we should cross to some actual place, which we could do anyhow if the labor were worth it; he means some fabulous yonder, something unknown to us" (*CS* 457). But the truth to which such figurative pronouncements point remains unknown; the "sage" cannot designate it more precisely: "All these parables really set out to say merely that the incomprehensible is incomprehensible, and we know that already" (ibid.). All parables, all literary texts thus boil down to a single tautology. Never has truth been sacrificed, to use Benjamin's words, in a more absolute sense.

The way the many—one could say endless—attempts at transmitting it must all invariably fail, the way the various comments, to quote the priest once again, only express the commentator's despair in the face of the unalterable Scriptures, is beautifully enacted in an earlier short piece entitled "Prometheus" (1918):

> There are four legends concerning Prometheus:
> According to the first he was clamped to a rock in the Caucasus for betraying the secrets of the gods to men, and the gods sent eagles to feed on his liver, which was perpetually renewed.
> According to the second Prometheus, goaded by the pain of the tearing beaks, pressed himself deeper and deeper into the rock until he became one with it.
> According to the third his treachery was forgotten in the course of thousands of years, forgotten by the gods, the eagles, forgotten by himself.
> According to the fourth everyone grew weary of the mean-

ingless affair. The gods grew weary, the eagles grew weary, the wound closed wearily.

There remained the inexplicable mass of rock. The legend tried to explain the inexplicable. As it came out of a substratum of truth it had in turn to end in the inexplicable. (*CS* 432)

The four legends "are," in the present, on paper, but what they "tried" to do was in the past; for it is over, it has failed. They "tried to explain the inexplicable." First they did it most meaningfully, in the religious terms of crime and punishment; a full-blown theology was imposed on the "mass of rock" of being. Then theological certainty began to crumble: the Prometheus who became one with the rock was completely identifying with God's punitive will, but also cunningly trying to escape it. The last two legends are legends of withdrawal from meaning: first forgetting, which may still imply divine forgiveness, then weariness "of the meaningless affair." What a far cry from the aggressive sense making of the first legend!

IV The inexplicable mass of rock that remains in the end is the blank at the center of Kafka, the wall against which all his myths must break. It is the peculiar status of such myths, made only to be unmade, that defines Kafka's type of modernity. His modernity lies in his epistemological position and its formal consequences rather than in what is popularly associated with the Kafkaesque: the thematics of alienation and anxiety, the décor of labyrinthine corridors and offices, the prophecies of totalitarianism.

One cannot doubt the tremendous influence of the Kafkaesque in the latter, popular sense. Kafka's imagery has become the standard imagery of innumerable novels dealing with urban bureaucracy or fascist politics. This adoption of his settings, however, is often only skin deep. His real influence goes deeper and has to do, I believe, with epistemological aspects like those I have outlined.

I call writers who have been somehow touched by this kind of influence post-Kafkan writers. They are post-Kafkan not simply because they come after Kafka, but because this fact is important for understanding their work. They are all concerned in one way or another with the question of truth or theme and its transmissibility through narrative. They can no longer accept the automatic reduction of fiction to themes. They confront a brute and meaningless existence (Sartre) and let human words (Beckett) or objects (Ionesco) proliferate desperately around it. They feel that narrative itself, not only its theme, collapses (Beckett), that only material surfaces remain (Robbe-Grillet). When they cling to a human message, metaphysical (the Americans) or political (British antifascist novels), they must deconstruct it. But they are unable, or unwilling, to write the radically skeptical type of fiction that is Kafka's great contribution to modern literature. They cannot, or will not, bear too much unknowing, the withdrawal from all theme, the renunciation of all reason. They end with some comfort, however paradoxical: Camus's absurd, Borges's illusionistic mysticism, Agnon's Jewish tradition.

But while differing from their great precursor in this respect, their attempts at coping with his influence—with their anxiety of his influence, Harold Bloom would say—have proved highly conducive to the shaping of their own voices. This is "an act of creative correction,"[16] which, to be really fruitful, must always involve a misreading. The following chapters are meant to provide a partial map of some such misreadings.

2

Kafka's Insect and Sartre's Crab

My nightmares probably came from an apprehension of the mere bulk of life, the feeling that the world is so tightly crammed with solid, bulging objects that there is not enough room for all of them: a nightmare feeling powerfully conveyed in the stories of Franz Kafka.

—*Edwin Muir,* An Autobiography

I In *What is Literature?* Sartre speaks of a "precious encouragement" he derived from Kafka's books. It had to do with a new way he found in Kafka "of rendering the irreducible truth of appearances and of making felt beyond them another truth which will always be denied us."[1]

The truth of appearances and the other truth; one irreducible, the other denied us. These are the two poles between which Kafka's influence on the French seems to oscillate.[2] While Sartre himself, or Alain Robbe-Grillet, strongly leans toward the stark truth of appearances, Camus thinks that Kafka has defected to the other, lusher, more comforting side.

What is the "new way" in Kafka of rendering the one and making felt the other? Sartre tried to define it three years earlier in a review of Maurice Blanchot's novel *Aminadab*.[3] There he described Kafka, as well as Blanchot, in terms of the fantastic. The two realities—transcendental and human—were mentioned there, too, but the former, totally beyond our reach, was said to serve in Kafka only to set off "man's abandonment in the realm of the human." Kafka's version of the fantastic was thus "limited to expressing the human world" (*LPE* 63, 64). A ghost of transcendence hovers over this world only to shed a cold, strange light on human objects, acts, and ends:

> This brush is here in my hand. I have only to take it in order to brush my clothes. But just as I touch it, I stop. It is a brush seen from the outside; it is there, in all its contingency; it refers back to contingent ends, just as the white pebble which the ant stupidly drags towards its hole appears to human eyes . . . [Blanchot] tries to make us see *our* ends—those ends which are born of us and which give meaning to our lives—as *ends for other people*. We are shown only the external side of those alienated, petrified ends, the side facing outwards, the side which makes *facts* of them. They are petrified ends, invaded by materiality, ends that are observed before they are wanted. As a result, the means take on an independent existence. If it is no longer taken for granted that one must brush oneself every morning, the brush seems an undecipherable implement. (*LPE* 72–73; Sartre's italics)

The brush, seen in a transcendent light as undecipherable implement, is only one example of the overall collapse of ends-means relationships that marks the realm of the fantastic. In this upside-down realm "the soul takes the place of the body" and vice versa; ends are "crushed by their own means and [try] vainly to pierce the enormous layers of matter"; objects "reveal their own instrumentality, but with an indiscipline and disorderly power, a kind of coarse independence that suddenly snatches their end from us just when we think we have it fast" (*LPE* 62, 65). The examples Sartre selects are typically Kafkaesque: "the labyrinth of corridors, doors and staircases that lead to nothing, the signposts that point to nothing, the innumerable signs that line the roads and that mean nothing . . . messages without content, without messenger and without sender" (*LPE* 67). These are, to Sartre, so many variations on what he regards as the central fantastic theme: the revolt of means against ends (*LPE* 65).

To become truly fantastic this revolt must appear as normal: the reader must assume the point of view of the hero who, belonging to a fantastic world, is fantastic himself and is never surprised.

Kafka's Gregor Samsa or land surveyor are never surprised; they do not contemplate their upside-down world from the outside, but belong to it and find it as natural as the dream is, not to waking reason, but to the dreamer (*LPE* 65, 70).[4]

II   This is one reason why Sartre's own novel *Nausea*, published five years earlier, in 1938, does not belong to the fantastic. Much of what Sartre has to say about Kafka and Blanchot fits his own novel like a glove. There are no Kafkaesque labyrinths of corridors or staircases and no bureaucracy in *Nausea*, but the "enormous layers of matter" that rebel against human ends and notions are at the very core of Antoine Roquentin's nauseous "adventure." Roquentin, however, *is* surprised. His diary, indeed, is kept only to record the changes that he feels have been threatening the regularity of his familiar world ever since he wanted to throw a pebble into the sea and could not. For this and other reasons the story, though abounding with miraculous metamorphoses, is not at all what Sartre would call fantastic.

Otherwise, however, it is strikingly close to the world Sartre attributes to Kafka (and Blanchot). The topsy-turvy café that he describes in his review as illustrating the revolt of means—a café where tables, seats, glasses, mirrors, are divorced from their human ends as utensils and become raw matter (*LPE* 65)—could easily be Roquentin's favorite café, the Rendez-vous des Cheminots, dissolving into whirlpools of color and mist.[5] And the above-quoted brush, about to be picked up when one's hand stops in midair and one observes it in all its contingency, "just as the white pebble which the ant stupidly drags towards its hole appears to human eyes," cannot fail to remind one of the pebble that gives Roquentin his first taste of nausea, the "origin of this whole business" (*N* 175): "Saturday the children were playing ducks and drakes and, like them, I wanted to throw a stone into the sea. Just at that moment I stopped, dropped the stone and left. Probably I looked somewhat foolish or absent-minded, because the children laughed behind my back" (*N* 7–8).

Sartre stops and drops the brush; Roquentin stops and drops

the stone. Both experiences bear a striking resemblance to that of the philosopher in "The Top," a short text by Kafka from the year 1920:

> A certain philosopher used to hang about wherever children were at play. And whenever he saw a boy with a top, he would lie in wait. As soon as the top began to spin the philosopher went in pursuit and tried to catch it. He was not perturbed when the children noisily protested and tried to keep him away from their toy; so long as he could catch the top while it was still spinning, he was happy, but only for a moment; then he threw it to the ground and walked away. For he believed that the understanding of any detail, that of a spinning top, for instance, was sufficient for the understanding of all things. For this reason he did not busy himself with great problems, it seemed to him uneconomical. Once the smallest detail was understood, then everything was understood, which was why he busied himself only with the spinning top. And whenever preparations were being made for the spinning of the top, he hoped that this time it would succeed: as soon as the top began to spin and he was running breathlessly after it, the hope would turn to certainty, but *when he held the silly piece of wood in his hand, he felt nauseated.* The screaming of the children, which hitherto he had not heard and which now suddenly pierced his ears, chased him away, and he tottered like a top under a clumsy whip.[6]

In all three cases, objects used as means for human ends—brush, stone (as used in the game of ducks and drakes) and top—are suddenly "invaded by materiality." They take on an independent existence. Their habitual ends are crushed, trying vainly to pierce matter. The stone now is "flat and dry, especially on one side, damp and muddy on the other" (*N* 8). The top now is a "silly piece of wood." As a result, both Sartre's Roquentin and Kafka's philosopher feel nauseated. Both have tried to join the children in their game, have failed, and are booed by the children. The philosopher's act has been more explicitly philosophical, he wanted to use the top for induction, to understand it in order to understand all things.[7]

In the final analysis, however, Roquentin's ambition—and his failure—are no different. According to Iris Murdoch:

> The metaphysical doubt which seizes Roquentin . . . is the doubt out of which the problem of particularity and the problem of induction arise. The doubter sees the world of everyday reality as a fallen and bedraggled place—fallen out of the realm of being into the realm of existence. The circle does not exist; but neither does what is named by "black" or "table" or "cold." The relation of these words to their context of application is shifting and arbitrary. What *does* exist is brute and nameless, it escapes from the scheme of relations in which we imagine it to be rigidly enclosed, it escapes from language and science, it is more than and other than our description of it.[8]

III   The philosopher's and Roquentin's nausea vis-à-vis the brute and nameless[9] resembles the fit of seasickness that Joseph K. undergoes in *The Trial* (*T* 83). His seasickness is described also as dizziness and nausea[10] and is the result of being hurled out of one's "habitual life,"[11] the human ends and notions he must give up. So is another seasickness in Kafka, that of the Supplicant in the early story "Description of a Struggle" (1904–5). This is how the Fat Man in that story diagnoses the Supplicant's state:

> Isn't it something like a fever, a seasickness on land, a kind of leprosy? Don't you feel it's this very feverishness that is preventing you from being properly satisfied with the real name of things, and that now, in your frantic haste, you're just pelting them with any old names? You can't do it fast enough. But hardly have you run away from them when you've forgotten the names you gave them. The poplar in the fields, which you've called the "Tower of Babel" because you didn't want to know it was a poplar, sways again without a name, so you have to call it "Noah in his cups."[12]

And the Supplicant confirms that "around me things sink away like fallen snow, whereas for other people even a little liqueur glass stands on the table steady as a statue" (*CS* 34). So, exactly so, does the glass of beer for the other customers in the Café Mably, whereas for Roquentin, as for the Supplicant, it sinks away, loses its taken-for-granted solidity:

> I have been *avoiding* looking at this glass of beer for half an hour. I look above, below, right and left; but I don't want to see *it*. And I know very well that all these bachelors around me can be of no help: it is too late, I can no longer take refuge among them. They could come and tap me on the shoulder and say, "Well, what's the matter with that glass of beer?" It's just like all the others. It's bevelled on the edges, has a handle, a little coat of arms with a spade on it and on the coat of arms is written "Spartenbrau," I know all that, but I know there is something else. Almost nothing. But I can't explain what I see. To anyone. There: I am quietly slipping into the water's depths, towards fear. (*N* 16–17; Sartre's italics)

To avoid slipping toward fear the Supplicant frantically "pelts" things with "any old names." The metaphorization of things, calling the poplar "Tower of Babel" or calling the moon, a few pages later, "forgotten paper lantern" (*CS* 41), is his way of controlling their threat by subjecting them to mind or to art. "Thinking about you," he tells them, "doesn't do you any good; you lose in courage and health" (*CS* 41). And this, I suppose, is why he celebrates the Drunk and the "quite unnatural odor of the dissolute Court of France" that surrounds him (*CS* 41). The divorce from reality that marks both the hallucinations of the Drunk and the precious make-believe world of the court, as well as the Supplicant's own metaphors, is an escape from threatening things: from the houses that collapse for no apparent reason, the spires that move in little circles, the lampposts that bend like bamboo (*CS* 35–36). It is an escape to artifice from a world that has lost its conceptual solidity and is now shifting and metamorphosing just like Roquentin's unveiled world.

But Roquentin, one could argue, rejects the kind of escape into words that is the Supplicant's way of coping with the fear of things. Isn't the existence he must face nameless by definition, ever escaping, as Iris Murdoch puts it, from language? "My words are dreams," he says (*N* 48). Moreover, the need to choose between living and telling (*N* 56) is a central preoccupation of his, and the rejection of narrative patterns ("beware of literature," *N* 79) explains much in *Nausea,* underlying Roquentin's abandonment of his historical work as well as his use of the diary form.

This is true, yet there is no simple opposition between the two texts. On the face of it, Roquentin's rejection of literature is diametrically opposed to the Supplicant's obsession with metaphors. But take Roquentin's climactic experience with the root of the chestnut tree: its antiverbal assertions ("I thought without words," *N* 173) are subverted by highly verbal practice ("serpent or claw or root or vulture's talon," *N* 173). "A monstrous proliferation of metaphors," says a deconstructive critic about this episode, "is paradoxically poured into the hole of being in order to show how language falls away in the face of existence unveiled."[13]

Again, it is true that narrative structures, as illustrated by Balzac (*N* 66–71) or Stendhal (*N* 110), seem to be implicitly rejected by Roquentin when he juxtaposes them with unstructured mimesis. But will he not embrace fiction as redemption on the last page of his diary? There he will dream of a book, a story, "something that could never happen, an adventure." He will think of it as "beautiful and hard as steel." He will hope that "a little of its clarity might fall over my past" (*N* 237–38).

In "Description of a Struggle," on the other hand, the Supplicant's feverish attempt to dominate existence through language ends in disaster. Both he and the Fat Man are defeated. Even earlier the Fat Man's attitude to "telling" had been rather ambiguous. When the Supplicant told him an anecdote about a woman in the garden—an insignificant nonincident—he found it most remarkable and could not make head or tail of it (*CS* 34). His incredulity is reminiscent of Roquentin's wonder at the way people tell stories in a café: "I marvel at these young people: drinking their coffee, they tell clear, plausible stories. If they are asked what they did yesterday, they aren't embarrassed: they bring you up to date in a few words. If I were in their place, I'd fall over myself" (*N* 15). The Fat Man shares Roquentin's incredulity at the easy way people impose sensemaking structures on senseless experience. The implied confidence

in human notions is beyond him. He is at this point far from na-
ively believing that man can control things through language. And
although he finally accepts the anecdote and admires the woman in
it (*CS* 45), this is only after realizing that it has nothing to do with
the truth: "We're not aiming at any definite purpose or at the
truth" (ibid.).

Both "Description of a Struggle" and *Nausea* thus seem to
oscillate between living and telling, existence and art. A comparison between Sartre's novel and another Kafka story will shed
further light on this conflict.

IV   The nausea that is Roquentin's in *Nausea* is mainly the
reader's in Kafka's "The Metamorphosis." Samsa himself, touching
an itching place on his belly with one of his numerous legs, feels "a
cold shiver run through him" (*CS* 90). By and large, however, it is
rather the outside world—family, lodgers, reader—that is nauseated. One reader made no bones about it: "This exceptionally repulsive story," he wrote a friend, ". . . it is infinitely repulsive." The
reader was Kafka, and the friend his fiancée Felice.[14]

There is a rare passage in *Nausea*, too, where the disgust is the
world's, not Roquentin's. This passage could easily pass for a
quotation from "The Metamorphosis" rewritten in the first person:

> I cross the room in the midst of silence. No one is eating: they
> are watching me, they have lost their appetite. . . . I leave.
> Now the colour will come back to their cheeks, they'll begin to
> jabber . . . they are watching my back with surprise and dis-
> gust; they thought I was like them, that I was a man, and I
> deceived them. I suddenly lost the appearance of a man and
> they saw a crab running backwards out of this human room.
> Now the unmasked intruder has fled: the show goes on. (*N*
> 166–67)

Replace "crab" with "insect" and this could easily pass for an interior monologue of Samsa's as he retreats after one of his attempts
to break back into the world. The components are strikingly similar: man metamorphosed into animal, stunned onlookers, retreat

from room, life going on after intruder's retreat. There follows, moreover, a description of a holiday atmosphere on the beach, with spring and sun and lightly dressed women (*N* 167), that is reminiscent of the heartless picnic with which "The Metamorphosis" ends (*CS* 139): the world thrives as the intruder disappears.

There is, of course, a vast difference between the two texts. Its most obvious indication is the third person used by Kafka as compared to the first person used by Sartre. Samsa's metamorphosis, emphatically not the figment of his imagination ("it was no dream," *CS* 89), is transformed in Roquentin into a mental "adventure." Roquentin's nausea therefore is his, not the world's, even when he projects it on others, as in the above-quoted passage. We have to do with his diary, with his consciousness, with the *realité humaine,* not with any outside change in things ("I think I'm the one who has changed," *N* 12). This is why *Nausea,* unlike "The Metamorphosis," is not a metaphysical tale or image but "a philosophical analysis which makes use of a metaphysical image."[15] It belongs to psychological realism, not to the metaphysical fantastic. Or, to put it in the terms coined by Tzvetan Todorov in his *Introduction à la littérature fantastique,* it belongs to *l'étrange* rather than to the *merveilleux:* what seems supernatural in it can be referred to dream, hallucination, or any other realistic explanation rather than be taken literally.[16]

Nevertheless, the two texts shed much light on each other. Perhaps they do so precisely because they are at once so similar and so dissimilar.

I have mentioned Samsa's cold shiver when his leg touches his belly. He draws the leg back immediately. What he does is no different from what Sartre does when he touches the brush and stops, or Roquentin when he holds the stone and drops it. Samsa, too, must suddenly face a world in which coarse matter has become independent, except that in his case it is his own body. It is his body that has undergone a metamorphosis from the human and functional to the beastly and senseless—the change undergone in *Nausea* by the seat in the tramway or the root of the chestnut tree. It is his body that defies its subservience to the human soul and threatens to crush it with its enormous layers of matter, to take its place (*LPE* 65), to overflood it with its animality and make it entirely beastly ("entière-ment brute"), like the root of the chestnut tree (*N* 171). But Sartre also includes bodies, including Roquentin's, in the latter's "adven-ture." Body, to Sartre, belongs to matter, to the *en-soi;* it is a thing, other than the *realité humaine* of consciousness. Bodies, therefore, like things, are constantly depersonalized in *Nausea;* fragmented, their fragments become independent, are defamiliarized and meta-morphosed. Thus, the hands of the woman in the Café Mably—her hands, not herself—smooth her blouse, straighten her hat, then stop, then move along her blouse and over her neck like large spiders (*N* 99). Or Roquentin's own body "slowly turns eastward, oscillates a little and begins to walk" (*N* 214). Particularly close to "The Meta-morphosis" is the sense of an alienated, animal body that Roquentin has when the adventure of existence floods over him and fills him:

> I see my hand spread out on the table. It lives—it is me. It opens, the fingers open and point. It is lying on its back. It shows me its fat belly. It looks like an animal turned upside down. The fingers are the paws. I amuse myself by moving them very rapidly, like the claws of a crab which has fallen on its back.
>
> The crab is dead: the claws draw up and close over the belly of my hand. . . . My hand turns over, spreads out flat on its stomach, offers me the sight of its back. A silvery back, shining a little—like a fish except for the red hairs on the knuckles. I feel my hand. I am these two beasts struggling at the end of my arms. My hand scratches one of its paws with the nail of the other paw. (*N* 134)

V   It is again into a crab that Roquentin is metamorphosed here. Many of the metamorphoses he experiences—either in his own body or in other people and things—are changes into aquatic and amphibious animals: jellyfish (*N* 27), sea lion (*N* 174), sea ele-phant (*N* 233), but above all the backward-running crab (*N* 17, 83, 134, 167). It is the regressive, primal aspect of "existence" that these creatures related to the primal waters indicate,[17] the retreat from human categories to sheer matter, the "slipping into the water's depths" as Roquentin puts it in the above-quoted passage about the glass of beer. But there are also ants, ringworm (*N* 83), and insects (*N* 179). In a particularly monstrous nightmare of metamorphoses somebody, feeling soemthing scratching in his mouth, goes to the mirror, opens his mouth—"and his tongue is an enormous, live centipede, rubbing its legs together and scraping his palate. He'd like to spit it out, but the centipede is a part of him" (*N* 212–13). Later on the same page men run through the streets, "open-mouthed, with their insect-tongue flapping its wings."

It is not only the insect itself that refers us to Kafka, but the posture of Roquentin's metamorphosed hand: it is a crab lying on its back, just like Samsa in the opening lines of "The Metamorphosis." This posture, too, is related to the primal: to a baby helplessly lying on its back, a woman ready to conceive. Thus, the child's hand in the library, about to be "violated" by the Autodidacte's thick finger, is "resting on its back, relaxed, soft and sensual" and has "the indolent nudity of a woman sunning herself after bathing" (*N* 221). But the same posture is also related to death. The crab, which is Roquentin's hand, is dead. So is the donkey lying on its back and carried down the river—the seat in the tramway as metamorphosed in Roquentin's mind. Divorced from its name and human end, seen, like the brush, from the outside in all its contingency, the seat becomes the bloated belly of a dead donkey turned upward, with thousands of little red paws in the air (*N* 169). The "primal waters" in which the crab lives and on which the donkey's corpse floats combine origin with death, drowning with obstinate rebirth. The insect fallen on its back serves, in another place, as image for this endless, senselessly recurrent struggle to exist: "But why, I thought, why so many existences, since they all look alike? What good are so many duplicates of trees? So many existences missed, obstinately begun again and again missed—*like the awkward efforts of an insect fallen on its back*? (I was one of those efforts)" (*N* 179; my italics). The insect on its back here spells a regression to what precedes existence itself: beyond the return to sex and death, to the contingency of nameless existence, it reaches back to the primal convulsions of preexistent matter struggling to be born into existence. Roquentin's experience here goes beyond the unveiling of existence to the most fundamental of all fundamental questions: Why existence?

This is the furthest point Roquentin reaches in his movement away from "normal" thought. The onlookers watching with surprise and disgust as the crab runs backward out of the "human room" are surprised and disgusted at the attempt to think nonhumanly. Like the children on the beach, they follow the rules of the human game, never stopping to observe the stone, never facing naked existence. Roquentin's insistence on stopping to observe, on seeing human objects and ends from the outside and finding them contingent, is a threat to their lives.

Their lives are anything but contingent. They are marked, on the contrary, by the necessity of rights and duties, of authority and tradition as embodied in the portraits at the Bouville Museum (*N* 112–29). That "the essential thing is contingency," that "all is free," is what they "try to hide from themselves with their idea of their rights" (*N* 176–77).

There is much in common between these respectable citizens, disgusted at the crab in their midst, and Gregor Samsa's father or, for that matter, any of Kafka's father figures. Of Jean Pacôme, one of the "leaders" looking down from the walls of the Bouville Museum, Roquentin writes that "the beating of his heart and the mute rumblings of his organs . . . assumed the form of rights to be instantly obeyed" (*N* 116). He had always insisted on his rights—"as a father, the right to be venerated; as a leader, the right to be obeyed without a murmur" (ibid.). Another member of the Pacôme family, like Bendemann's father in "The Judgement," seems to pass judgment on Roquentin, and "his judgement went through me like a sword and questioned my very right to exist. And it was true, I had always realized it; I hadn't the right to exist" (*N* 115–16), for Roquentin, like Bendemann or Samsa or K., is "neither father, nor grandfather, not even a husband" (*N* 118). No wonder one of Olivier Blévigne's (another "leader") volumes of collected speeches is called *The Duty to Punish* and seems to be much in demand, for it is out of print (*N* 126).

The fathers and leaders—in both *Nausea* and "The Metamorphosis"—are diametrically opposed to metamorphosis. They stand for tradition and solidity. They "aren't afraid," for they have never faced unveiled existence. Their water is trained and runs from taps, their light fills bulbs when you turn on the switch; their world obeys fixed, unchangeable laws (*N* 211). Roquentin, like Samsa, "belongs to another species": he sees "great, vague nature"; he knows it has no laws; he knows that what his fathers and leaders take for constancy can change tomorrow (*N* 211–12).

That the fathers are subject to change and disintegration is shown by Doctor Rogé. Doctor Rogé is a "rock" (*N* 96) of self-assertion. He is the essence of traditionalism, always transforming his past into wisdom. Grotesquely fat, like the Fat Man in "Description of a Struggle," he, too, closes his eyes to reality. And if the Fat Man finally appears as "a yellow wooden idol which had become useless" (*CS* 28) and drowns, Doctor Rogé's face finally becomes "a cardboard mask." "This man is going to die soon," writes Roquentin (*N* 96).

VI In addition to the sudden confrontation with unveiled existence and the subsequent estrangement from an outraged environment, *Nausea* shares with "The Metamorphosis" a concept of music as redemption. Music points the way to the "unknown nourishment" Samsa craves and never gets (*CS* 131); it belongs to the "other world" that Roquentin "can see in the distance, but without ever approaching it" (*N* 234). Music, that is, represents transcendence, that "other truth which will always be denied us." To the insect Samsa transcendence appears as food; to the man Roquentin it appears as a distant view, not unlike the Castle to K., ever seen in the distance but never approached.

Music also appears to Roquentin in philosophical terms, quite unlike the instinctual nature it has for the insect. Roquentin platonically associates music with mathematics and with the necessity of being, as against the contingency of existence (*N* 172, 176, 179–80). The Jew who composed Roquentin's favorite song and the negress who sings it are saved, they have "washed themselves of the sin of existing" (*N* 236–37). Samsa's attraction to his sister's violin playing, on the other hand, is all instinct; "unknown" is the only (vaguely) philosophical term associated with it. What it does mainly is arouse aggressive and incestuous fantasies in Samsa (*CS* 131). At the same time this unknown nourishment definitely replaces in his mind the material nourishment he no longer wants. It therefore constitutes the opposite pole to his animal being: "Was he an animal, that music had such an effect upon him?" (*CS* 130). But the music that has such an effect upon him is rather poor. So it seems from the way the lodgers behave: they find Grete's violin playing neither good nor enjoyable and suffer it only out of courtesy (*CS* 130). The same holds for Roquentin's favorite song. It is neither the music of the spheres nor Bach. It is a far cry from the "pure and rigid lines" that Roquentin attributes to music (*N* 172). Its words, rather, bring it close to the "sin of existing": "Some of these days / You'll miss me, honey." Technically the song can be said to belong not to the real world but to what Sartre calls the realm of the "imaginary." In this sense it *is* beyond existence, showing the same sort of necessity that Bach would show, in that its sequence is necessarily the same, regardless of time and place.[18] Still, why should Sartre select a popular hit, blatantly tainted by worldly emotion, in order to illustrate the "other truth" of necessity and of music?

Both writers, it would therefore seem, have difficulty simply presenting music as redemption. They may both be said to ironize this romantic motif. Samsa's craving for the unknown nourishment, for the negation of animality, is partly subverted both by the poor quality of Grete's violin playing and by his own sadoerotic fantasies. The animal-spiritual dichotomy is thus problematized. The same holds for Sartre's distinction between life and art. The music that should represent art beyond life is deeply steeped in life.

Although the difficulty is similar, its roots seem to be different in the two writers. In Kafka's case it derives from his basic uncertainty about the ultimate meaning of things, and his ensuing refusal to present the reader with unambiguous truths. A bodiless, ecstatic attraction, in the insect, to higher music would imply that animality has been the route to purification and would turn the story into a mini-bildungsroman. Sartre, on the other hand, does not avoid definite meanings. His novel, after all, is a "philosophical analysis." He problematizes his own distinction between music (or literature) and existence not because he doubts that they really differ, but because the banishment of life from art goes against his grain. If living excludes telling, if the book contemplated by Roquentin must be limited to what could never happen, literature becomes a sort of Rilkean inwardness, renouncing the authenticity of consciousness in the world. By selecting "Some of these days," says Merleau-Ponty, Sartre "refused in advance the religion of art and its consolations. Man may get beyond his contingency in what he creates, but all expression, even what is known as Great Art, is an act born of man. The miracle takes place everywhere at ground-level, not in the privileged heaven of fine arts. The principles of order and disorder are one; the contingency of things and our liberty which dominates it are cut from the same cloth."[19]

Merleau-Ponty's fine rhetoric may blur the ambivalence of Sartre's attitude in *Nausea*. It is an ambivalence that will be solved, in *What is Literature?*, by the total divorce of prose from poetry, the limitation of prose to meaning and poetry to beauty. In *Nausea* Roquentin can still crave art beyond life, but he sees it embodied in "Some of these days," a hybrid of art *and* life.

What matters, however, is that writing, the free act of creation, is presented as a promise of deliverance at the end of the road. Roquentin has seen existence face-to-face, contingent and brute, its matter rebelling against human ends; but now he may try to write a book—a book that would be above existence, that would make people ashamed of their existence. "A little of its clarity," says Roquentin, "might fall over my past" (*N* 238).[20] The chaotic upside-down world of the fantastic would be redeemed by the order-making act of consciousness.

"The writer, a free man addressing free men," Sartre says in *What is Literature?*, "has only one subject—freedom."[21] Whatever this freedom may mean (there is a "stupefying ambiguity" in Sartre's use of the word),[22] it cannot but strike us as the very opposite of Kafka's necessity. Kafka, a doomed man addressing doomed men, has only one subject—doom. Samsa's experience, analogous to Roquentin's, though on its own absolutely different level, can never end in a free activity of consciousness. It must end in its extinction.

3

Sisyphus and Prometheus: Camus and Kafka

I "Shame" and "execration" are the words with which Kafka's *The Trial* and Camus's *The Outsider* respectively end. The attitudes behind the two words, however, are very different. Meursault, the Outsider, happily hopes for those howls of execration to greet him on his day of execution. Joseph K., "like a dog," feels that the shame of it will outlive him.

The ultimate victory that Camus seems to pit against Joseph K.'s ultimate humiliation is indicative of the philosophical and temperamental differences between the two writers. In spite of the great affinity critics have found between them, Camus seems rather ambivalent in his attitude to Kafka's work. In an essay on Melville he speaks of the "monotony" of Kafka's "modes of expression and invention," of his being "cut off from flesh or nature."[1] In a preface to Roger Martin du Gard's collected work, Camus complains that the visionary in Kafka gained the upper hand over the artist, and he deplores Kafka's influence on contemporary writing. It is an influence, he says, that has joined that of Dostoyevsky in replacing characterization in depth by the use of character as a mere carrier of a "spiritual dimension": "Des ombres passionnées ou inspirées y tracent le commentaire gesticulant d'une reflexion sur la destinée."[2] A similar reference to Kafka's "inspired automata" is made in "Hope and the Absurd in the Work of Franz Kafka," Camus's most elaborate critique of Kafka's work.[3]

Before turning to this essay, highly revealing in its insights and particularly in its misunderstandings, let us recall some obvious affinities between *The Trial* and *The Outsider* that have made the comparison between the two writers so natural. Meursault (a name sometimes used by Camus himself as a pseudonym[4] and thus reminiscent of Kafka's use of his own initial) is thirty years old[5] like Joseph K., and, like him, an insignificant clerk. Both lead rather unfeeling lives, their lack of feeling highlighted by superficial love affairs. Both are arrested and finally executed (or are about to be). Toward the end both must face a prison chaplain, an encounter that in both novels is described in great detail and has central significance.

In addition, critics noticed from the start an affinity in technique. They felt that Hemingway and Kafka had combined to make Camus the sort of "objective" writer he was. But Sartre, in a review of *The Outsider,* strongly disagreed. He thought, indeed, that Kafka and Camus were rather diametrically opposed to one another: "What is this new technique? 'It's Kafka written by Hemingway,' I was told. I confess that I have found no trace of Kafka in it. M. Camus' views are entirely of this earth, and Kafka is the novelist of impossible transcendence; for him, the universe is full of signs that we cannot understand; there is a reverse side to the décor. For M. Camus, on the contrary, the tragedy of human existence lies in the absence of any transcendence." He then adds that Camus, drenched in the Algerian sun and summer, "is as far removed as possible from the anguish of a Kafka."[6]

The two contrasts Sartre draws—immanence versus transcendence and sunniness versus anguish—are related. Kafka's anguish derives from the ever-present threat of an inaccessible judging authority, while Camus's cheerfulness—not only his awareness of the "tragedy of human existence"—has to do with the absence, to him, of such authority and the resulting sense of mastery over his life. Transcendence to Kafka is a source of anguish; immanence to Camus is a source of exaltation. But that is not exactly how Camus himself sees it.

Camus's notion of immanence, of being "entirely of this earth" as Sartre puts it, and, on the other hand, his view of Kafka's transcendence can be learned from his *Myth of Sisyphus,* indispensable for understanding both his essay on Kafka and *The Outsider.*[7] I shall limit myself to some points in *The Myth* that are directly relevant to the relation between the two writers.

Man, according to *The Myth,* is placed in the insolubly tragic situation of confronting an irrational world while longing wildly for rational clarity. This is Camus's "absurd." It "is not in man . . . nor in the world, but in their presence together" (*MS* 23). It is "that divorce between the mind that desires and the world that disappoints, my nostalgia for unity, this fragmented universe and the contradiction that binds them together" (*MS* 37). The absurd is the irreconcilability of two certainties—"my appetite for the absolute and for unity and the impossibility of reducing this world to a rational and reasonable principle" (*MS* 38).

Living in this contradiction with perfect lucidity, with a stubborn refusal to delude oneself, is the desideratum. But man, it seems, cannot bear too much absurdity. *The Myth of Sisyphus* is above all directed against those existentialists, whether religious or atheistic, who cannot "live with [their] ailments," who "want to be cured" (*MS* 29) and therefore "leap" to an absolute beyond reason, either God or history.[8] They "deify what crushes them and find reason to hope in what impoverishes them" (*MS* 24). They make up a "metaphysic of consolation" (*MS* 34). Camus's idea of the opposition between existential and absurd is succinctly summed up with reference to the religious existentialist Shestov: "To Shestov reason is useless but there is something beyond reason. To an absurd mind reason is useless and there is nothing beyond reason" (*MS* 27).

Although Camus does not mention Kafka in *The Myth* itself, he clearly regards him, as transpires from the appended essay about him, as one of those religious existentialists who cannot bear too much reality. Or rather, at first he could; *The Trial*, says Camus, *is* an absurd novel. But later, in *The Castle*, he could not help but make the illegitimate leap to God:

> The more truly absurd *The Trial* is, the more moving and illegitimate the impassioned "leap" of *The Castle* seems. But we find here again in a pure state the paradox of existential thought as it is expressed, for instance, by Kierkegaard: "Earthly hope must be killed; only then can one be saved by true hope," which can be translated: "One has to have written *The Trial* to undertake *The Castle*." . . . the absurd work itself may lead to the infidelity I want to avoid. The work which was but an ineffec-

tual repetition of a sterile condition, a lucid glorification of the ephemeral, becomes here a cradle of illusions. It explains, it gives a shape to hope. . . . Kafka refuses his god moral nobility, evidence, virtue, coherence, but only the better to fall into his arms. The absurd is recognized, accepted, and man is resigned to it, but from then on we know that it has ceased to be the absurd. (*MS* 99–100)

Kafka's infinitely painful obsession with a terrifying transcendence, which never stopped haunting his life and work, is thus reduced by Camus to a comforting illusion into which he "leapt" to be saved. For he apparently lacked Camus's own lucidity, his own heroic capacity for living without hope.

II   There is much in Camus's essay that illuminates Kafka: his "perpetual oscillations between the natural and the extraordinary" (*MS* 94), the way "the absurd effect is linked to an excess of logic" (*MS* 96), his openness to many interpretations. This last point, however, with which the essay both begins and ends, makes Camus's misreading the more striking. For, on one hand, he concludes the last footnote with the splendid words: "It is the fate and perhaps the greatness of [Kafka's] work that it offers everything and confirms nothing" (*MS* 102). But on the other hand, he judges that work as if its theological purport were to be taken for granted. *The Castle,* he says, "is first of all the individual adventure of a soul in quest of its grace, of a man who asks of this world's objects their royal secret and of women the signs of the god that sleeps in them" (*MS* 94). It is a novel about "nostalgia for a lost paradise" (*MS* 97), its characters "utterly consigned to the humiliations of the divine" (*MS* 98). In *The Castle* "there is nothing that is not God's" (*MS* 98).

Now, first of all, the very presence of a "quest" or "nostalgia" should not, in Camus's own terms, exclude the absurd. Doesn't he insist, on the contrary, that the absurd is the tension, the divorce, between our nostalgia for rational understanding and the irrational world that is bound to disappoint it? One must not, he says, "suppress the absurd by denying one of the terms of its equation" (*MS* 37). *The Castle,* therefore, may be a novel about nostalgia for a lost, meaningful, unified world and still be an absurd novel, for it certainly does not suppress the other term: the world never ceases to disappoint K. He never gets to the Castle.

Camus's assertion, therefore, that while *The Trial* "propounds a problem," "describes . . . without concluding," and "diagnoses," *The Castle* "solves," "explains," and "imagines a treatment" (*MS* 96–97), is most extraordinary. If anything, *The Castle* is less explicable than its predecessor. It can be said to "imagine a treatment" only by a reader who accepts without reservation, indeed simplifies, Max Brod's interpretation of the novel as a theological allegory. If *The Castle* is the story of a man in quest of grace, then it may "solve" the problem *The Trial* propounds: Is man subjected to God's law? Why, let him pray for grace. But Brod's interpretation, though perhaps "offered" by the text, is never "confirmed" by it. It is perhaps somewhat corroborated by external evidence, notably by some of Kafka's aphorisms about what he calls the "indestructible." But there is no telling in the novel itself whether the quest is for God, for evil, or (as Camus wants it) for an evil God, a God without "moral nobility, evidence, virtue, coherence" (*MS* 100); or, for that matter, whether the quest is for religious or moral certainty at all, rather than for an inaccessible sex object or for unreachable integration in society, and so on. "The greatness of that work," one is tempted to remind Camus of his own words, is "that it offers everything and confirms nothing." Its greatness, in other words, is that it keeps pointing to a doctrine but has lost it. This unique status has made it the symptomatic work of its age. It neither "solves" nor "explains," let alone "leaps" to God.[9]

III   One could argue further that of the two writers, the one really incapable of living with his ailments and without hope is Camus himself. This transpires from the way *The Outsider* ends, as well as from the figure of the mythical Sisyphus in *The Myth of Sisyphus.*

That Meursault is the embodiment of Absurd Man, and that

The Myth can serve as a running commentary on *The Outsider,* is manifest enough. Quotations from *The Myth* often sound like annotations to *The Outsider.* Thus, the discovery of the void—located, by the way, in *The Myth,* too, around the age of thirty (*MS* 10)—shows in "replying 'nothing' when asked what one is thinking about" (*MS* 10), which is, of course, a habit with Meursault. He thinks about nothing because, as Absurd Man, he is "forever a stranger to himself" (*MS* 15). He refuses to speak to Marie of love because, as Absurd Man, he knows that "we call love what binds us to certain creatures only by reference to a collective way of seeing for which books and legends are responsible. But of love [he] know[s] only that mixture of desire, affection, and intelligence that binds [him] to this or that creature" (*MS* 54–55). He is aware, that is, of the fragmentariness of the universe; he abandons unity and glorifies diversity (*MS* 86). He will not mourn for his mother or regret having killed the Arab, for the absurd "restores to remorse its futility" (*MS* 50), "rejects regret, that other form of hope" (*MS* 54), shows that "there may be responsible persons, but there are no guilty ones" (*MS* 50). He hurls insults at the prison chaplain and his heavenly consolations, for "the Absurd. . . does not lead to God" (*MS* 30). Instead, it thrives on the indifference of a godless universe: "At last man will again find in [this mad world] the wine of the absurd and the bread of indifference on which he feeds his greatness" (*MS* 39)—words that cannot but remind us of *The Outsider:* "for the first time, the first, I laid my heart open to the benign indifference of the universe" (*O* 120).

In both cases the world's indifference to human hopes is a source of joy. Surrounded by the gray stone walls,[10] Meursault now realizes that he has been happy and that he is happy still (*O* 120). Though "emptied of hope," he can still wish that on the day of his execution he will be greeted with the huge crowd's howls of execration.

Similarly, the mythical Sisyphus—Camus's prototype of the Absurd Man—"must be imagined happy" (*MS* 91). His lucidity and consciousness of hopelessness lend joy to his eternal descent to the plain. Yes, joy: "this word is not too much" (*MS* 90). "Happiness and the absurd are two sons of the same earth" (ibid.).

One finds it hard to see why this happiness and joy is less of an escape than what Camus finds in existential philosophy (*MS* 24). Do not Meursault and Sisyphus, too, "find reason to hope in what impoverishes them" (ibid.)? Don't they also "integrate the absurd and in that communion cause to disappear its essential character, which is opposition, laceration and divorce" (*MS* 26)? "In his failure," Camus quotes Kierkegaard, "the believer finds his triumph" (*MS* 28). Isn't this precisely what Meursault and Sisyphus also do?

It seems that Camus's presentation of the two poles—the absurd and the existential, Meursault and K.—could easily be turned upside down. Kafka could be shown to be the one capable of facing the hopeless truth of guilt and defeat, while Camus could be shown to "leap" into the illusion of revolt, lucidity, and joy. The way the two writers handle two figures of Greek myth will make this clearer. I am referring to Camus's Sisyphus and Kafka's Prometheus (*CS* 432).

The two legends have several elements in common. Both heroes stole the gods' secrets, passed them on to man, and were punished (*MS* 88). The punishment in both cases involves a rock—Prometheus is clamped to a rock, Sisyphus must roll a rock up to the top of a mountain. Like Prometheus in the second of the legends mentioned by Kafka, Camus's Sisyphus nearly turns into stone himself ("A face that toils so close to stones is already stone itself," *MS* 89). And the punishment in both cases is eternal: the eagles eternally feed on Prometheus's liver, which is perpetually renewed; the stone eternally falls back to the plain and must be rolled up again.

These similarities, however, only accentuate the wide gap separating the two writers. The heroic, humanistic "crime" is followed, in Camus, by a heroic response to the punishment: lucidity, hopelessness, scorn. Sisyphus is "superior to his fate," "stronger than his rock," "master of his days." In Kafka the heroic crime, as well as the very pattern of crime and punishment, gradually dissolve into meaninglessness. The four legends about Prometheus are withdrawn, as we have seen, one by one, and only the "inexplicable mass of rock" remains.

Luckily, we have a short portrait of Prometheus by Camus, too. His Prometheus, it turns out, is Sisyphus's twin brother: "The enchained hero maintains, amid the thunder and lightning of the Gods, his quiet faith in man. This is how he is harder than his rock and more patient than his vulture. More than his rebellion against the gods, it is this long stubbornness which is meaningful for us."[11] This meaningful stubbornness is the very denial of Kafka's inexplicable mass of rock. Humanistic faith is Camus's "metaphysic of consolation."

IV   It is in the light of this philosophical diagreement that the apparent technical affinity between *The Trial* and *The Outsider* must be considered. Sartre, we have seen, denies there is such an affinity and goes on to contrast Kafka's "impossible transcendence" with Camus's "absence of any transcendence." He then dismisses the importance of Hemingway's influence as well, but agrees that Camus makes use of an "American technique," which he describes with reference to a quotation from *The Myth:* "A man is talking on the telephone. We cannot hear him behind the glass partition, but we can see his senseless mimicry. We wonder why he is alive?" Sartre comments:

> M. Camus has a method ready to hand. He is going to insert a glass partition between the reader and his characters. Is there really anything sillier than a man behind a glass window? Glass seems to let everything through. It stops only one thing: the meaning of his gestures. The glass remains to be chosen. It will be the Outsider's mind, which is really transparent, since we see everything it sees. However, it is so constructed as to be transparent to things and opaque to meanings.[12]

This seems an excellent metaphor for the effect of Camus's technique. Is it Kafkaesque as well as American? Joseph K.'s consciousness, no less than Meursault's seems transparent to things (the warders' outfits, the offices and corridors) and opaque to meanings. What is the trial about? What is Joseph K.'s guilt? It is opaque even to the meanings of his own gestures. Both Meursault and Joseph K. seem to have no access to their own inner beings. And since *The Trial* is largely restricted to Joseph K.'s—and *The Outsider* to Meursault's—perspective, both novels fall, as it were, between two stools. Both relinquish omniscience, or even partial rectification of their dominant perspective through other perspectives, but also the advantages of introspection. Thus, they seem to share a double effect of truncatedness. Its raison d'être, however, is very different in each case, and the difference has to do with the philosophical difference I have been describing.

Kafka, we know, wrote forty-two pages of *The Castle* in the first person before he switched to the third person. The revisions he consequently had to make in the first forty-two pages were minimal. They consisted almost exclusively in replacing the first-person pronoun by the third person.[13] The narrative, that is, continued to be largely restricted to K.'s consciousness even after the switch to the third person.

This textual history of *The Castle* can serve as an illustration to Gérard Genette's argument as formulated by Shlomith Rimmon-Kenan, that "there is no difference in perspective between a first person narrative and a third person center of consciousness: both are interior and both have a character as a focus."[14] Switching from first to third person, Kafka did not have to switch to a different perspective. K. was still his focus, though the narrator—and that is precisely Genette's point—did change. Narrator and perspective—or, to use Genette's terminology, voice and focus—were no longer of the same origin. They became separate.

Why did Kafka wish to separate them? Why did he prefer a narrator who did not take part in the story to one who did? Dorrit Cohn suggests he did so because of the difficulty of using the first person while avoiding access to inner thoughts and emotions.[15] Take, for example, K.'s first meeting with his "assistants": " 'Who are you?' he asked, looking from one to the other. 'Your assistants,' they answered. . . . 'What?' said K., 'are you my old assistants whom I told to follow me and whom I am expecting?' They answered in the affirmative. 'That's good,' observed K. after a short pause. 'I'm glad you've come.' 'Well,' he said, after another pause, 'you've come very late, you're very slack' " (*C* 23–24). Were this written in the first person with K. as narrator, the result would have been embarrassing. A first-person narrator who would quote himself and speak of the pauses between his sentences without betraying the thoughts that had given rise to those pauses would strike one as either exceptionally lacking in self-knowledge or pathologically suspicious of the reader. When Kafka switched to the third person he saved K. from this personal oddity—not because he didn't want him to be odd, but because his oddity would have been irrelevant. The dissociation from the inner life was not meant to be a psychological matter. It had nothing to do with the specific makeup of the character K. It was meant to be an epistemological problem, belonging to man as such and now enacted in a narrative technique that combined a third-person center of consciousness with an external focus motivated by the presence of an external narrator. The external focus could be derived from a voice other than K.'s rather than from an anomalous split in K.'s own perspective. It was the text now, not K., that fell between the two stools of character as focus and narrator as focus, "enjoying" a double ignorance: both of a character who can see only what he can see, and an external narrator who cannot—or will not—see through the character.[16]

Not so Camus. The oddity of a first-person narrator who is outside his thoughts and feelings did not deter him; it was precisely what he was after. For wasn't the Outsider his subject? The Outsider was outside all "normal" feeling and could therefore go through the motions, the physical gestures, of socially accepted conduct without ever experiencing the emotions behind them. He could follow the Warden to the mortuary, for instance, though feeling no real need to see his mother for the last time (*O* 15). He could quote himself—or rather his silences—without ever indicating that they stood for anything: "Noticing that I said nothing, he added that . . . " (*O* 37); "I just listened, without speaking" (*O* 38); "When I didn't say anything, he asked me . . ." (*O* 40); "I kept silence and he said it again" (*O* 40). Or he could explicitly say that feelings mean nothing to him: "A moment later she asked me if I loved her. I said that sort of question had no meaning" (*O* 42). "He went on to ask me if I had felt grief on that 'sad occasion.' . . . I answered that in recent years I'd rather lost the habit of noting my feelings, and hardly knew what to answer. I could truthfully say I'd been quite fond of Mother—but really that didn't mean much" (*O* 68–69).

The Outsider was precisely the man who suffered an incompatibility—or, as Absurd Man, had the privilege of being aware of the incompatibility—between socially accepted behavior and inner emptiness, between what one was expected to think and feel and what one actually thought and felt (or rather didn't think and didn't feel). This inner split could only be expressed by presenting Meursault himself as detached from a supposed inwardness, a stranger to the socially acceptable self, going through the motions of emotional life but not really experiencing it until no longer able even to go through its motions: by making Meursault himself the narrator of his own story.

I would add parenthetically, therefore, that I cannot agree with Genette's claim that *The Outsider* shows a paradoxical technique of internal narration combined with external focalization.[17] The reader's unfamiliarity with Meursault's inner life derives not from an external focus that cannot fathom it, but from Meursault's own "uncomprehending and disjointed narrative viewpoint," his "world of incoherence, a world where rational analysis has little scope and where moral purposes and responses are conspicuously absent."[18] It seems to me that the formulation Genette rejects— "interior focalization with an almost total paralipsis of thoughts"[19] —is more to the point.

V   Sartre's description of Camus's technique in terms of a glass partition calls now for some qualification. Genette rightly complains that it is ambiguous, for "it does not tell on which side of the glass window Meursault is—or, if we abandon the metaphor, whether the opacity of his mind to meanings refers to reception or to transmission."[20] If it is "between the reader and his characters" that the partition is inserted, the opacity is of transmission. But if, as seems from the latter part of the quotation, it is Meursault's own mind that is transparent to things and opaque to meanings, the opacity is inherent to Meursault. He can perceive the objects of the world in great physical detail but is blind to meanings, to fixed concepts, to stable patterns of unity. Perhaps "blind" is misleading: to Camus he is the Seer, the Outsider who sees the truth of the absurd.

In *The Rebel*, published nine years after Sartre's review of *The Outsider*, Camus himself uses the glass window metaphor. Interestingly, it is used to describe the "American technique" with which Sartre, in the same review, had associated him:

> The American novel claims to find its unity in reducing man either to elementals or to his external reactions and to his behaviour. It does not choose feelings or passions of which to give a detailed description, such as we find in classic French literature. It rejects analysis and the search for a fundamental psychological motive which could explain and recapitulate the behaviour of a character. . . . Its technique consists of describing men by their outside appearances, in their most casual actions, of reproducing, without comment, everything they say down to their repetitions and finally by acting as if men were entirely defined by their daily automatisms. On this mechanical level men, in fact, seem exactly alike, which explains this peculiar universe in which all the characters appear interchangeable, even down to their physical peculiarities. . . . it is perfectly obvious that this fictitious world is not attempting a reproduction, pure and simple, of reality, but the most arbitrary form of stylization. It is born of a mutilation and of a voluntary mutilation performed on reality. The unity thus obtained is a degraded unity, a levelling off of human beings and of the world. It would seem that, for these writers, it is the inner life which deprives human actions of unity and which tears people away from one another. This is a partially legitimate suspicion. But rebellion which is one of the sources of the art of fiction, can only find satisfaction in constructing unity on the basis of affirming this interior reality and not of denying it. . . . This type of novel, purged of interior life, in which *men seem to be observed behind a pane of glass*, logically

ends by giving itself, as its unique subject, the supposedly aver-
age man studied from the pathological point of view . . . [a]
despairing world in which wretched automatons live in the
most mechanically coherent way and which American novelists have presented as a heart rending but sterile protest.[21]

Both the subject—the American novel—and the use of the
glass window metaphor relate Camus's words to Sartre's, and implicitly reject the latter. No, he seems to be replying to Sartre, I'm
not making use of the American technique, nor am I inserting a
glass partition between my characters and the reader. I find this
technique (with its use, one could add anachronistically, of external
focalization, as in Hemingway's "The Killers," which is Genette's
example), this suspension of the search for psychological motivation, this reduction of man to external gestures—I find it all a
mutilation performed on reality. The unity achieved by art must
affirm interior reality, not deny it.

This defense of the psychological approach throws light on
Camus's ambivalent attitude to Kafka. The "wretched automatons"
that inhabit the despairing world of the American novel remind
one of Camus's above-quoted description of Kafka's characters as
"inspired automata" or "inspired shadows." If the Americans reduce man to "elementals," Kafka, on the contrary, makes him a
carrier of a "spiritual dimension." In either case portraiture in
depth is lost; reality is flattened, purged of interior life. The round
realism of a Martin du Gard is favorably contrasted by Camus not
only with the Americans, but with Kafka as well.[22]

In the final analysis, therefore, I believe that Camus's treatment
of Meursault is consciously different from Kafka's treatment of
Joseph K. By not divulging Meursault's thoughts and feelings,
Camus does not leave out his interior life as irrelevant, but defines
it as absurd. Kafka wrote: "For the last time psychology!"[23] He is
after the more total vision of metaphysics. His radical imagination
conceives man's fate as having no connection with his inner *Einstel-
lung*. The priest's words to Joseph K.—"it is not necessary to accept everything as true, one must only accept it as necessary" (*T*

243)—wrest human life away from all graspable motivation and fling it back to the *Ananké* of the Greeks. All desire for motivation must end in the inexplicable mass of rock.

Camus's skepticism is much less radical. It applies to the "collective way of seeing" (*MS* 55), to the clichés our nostalgia for unity automatically imposes on fragmentary experience. It does not apply to the Outsider's way of seeing, to his acceptance of the void. This absurd way of seeing includes what *seems* like a Kafkaesque wholesale preclusion of interior reality, but is in fact a rejection of only that part of interior reality which conforms to the mendacious dictates of collective reason. When Meursault keeps silence, he does so not because his inner life as such is inaccessible but because he is a stranger to what the collective way of seeing expects one's inner life to be. As a stranger to the collective way of seeing, he can see the truth. Like Prometheus, he will maintain, amid the thunder and lightning of the gods, his quiet faith in man.

No wonder he can happily hope for the howls of execration to greet him on his day of execution. No wonder Joseph K., impotent, inconsolable victim of incomprehensible powers, feels that, like a dog, the shame of it will outlive him.

4

The Staircase and Where It Leads:
Robbe-Grillet and Kafka

I   If ever there was a literalist of the imagination, Alain Robbe-Grillet is one. In his essay "From Realism to Reality" he declares the sea gulls of his imagination, whose flight he had described in *The Voyeur,* to be more real than the sea gulls of the Brittany coast. But not, as one would expect, because the imagination has dissolved them into symbol, idea, or objective correlative, but because it has bestowed on them a literal material presence that "matters" because it is imagined: "They too had probably come, in one way or another, from the external world, and perhaps even from Brittany, but they had been transformed, and at the same time had seemed to become more real *because* they were now imaginary."[1] The products of the mind are more real than the outside world not because they are spiritual, exempt from matter and its vicissitudes, but because they are fictitious, that is, one's own. It is their very falseness, their being constructed by the mind, not a transcription of what is exterior to them, that makes them "matter." Once invented, no spiritual, symbolic meaning must be attached to, or expected from, them. They can now be simply observed in their full, invented glory: "A new sort of narrator has been born, here: he is not only a man who describes the things he sees, but he is at the same time a person who is inventing the things that surround him and seeing the things he is inventing." (*STNN* 157).

Such a new sort of narrator, says Robbe-Grillet, a "creator of a material world" par excellence, is Kafka (*STNN* 158). The narrator who observes an invented world and does not allegorize it seems indeed very close to Kafka as described by Walter Benjamin—a Kafka who "divests the human gesture of its traditional supports and then has a subject for reflection without end." Kafka, as Benjamin sees him, invents a world of gestures that one can contemplate forever, as pure presence. If Benjamin speaks of Kafka's gestic theater, a code of gestures with no symbolic meaning, Robbe-Grillet speaks of an irreducible gesture described by Kafka in his diary: "the peculiar, unfinished, awkward gesture made by someone passing by, which seems to have neither function nor precise intention" (*STNN* 158). Or he speaks of the movements of Kafka's heroes, "which are the only things Kafka makes us aware of, the only real things" (*STNN* 159).

Robbe-Grillet, like Benjamin, thus sees the divorce of the fictive material world from ultimate meaning as central to Kafka. For Benjamin, however, this divorce does not exclude a constant pointing toward an ever-elusive meaning. Kafka's stories, to him, are devoid of meaning but always aim at meaning. They are parables that enjoy the paradoxical status of not being parables and yet refusing "to be taken at their face value." To Robbe-Grillet, on the other hand, Kafka's parables are not parables and they *do* want to be taken at their face value. "The visible world of his novels," he says, "is certainly, for him, the real world, and what is behind it (if there is anything) seems to be valueless in comparison with the evidence of the objects, actions, words etc. . . . Perhaps Kafka's staircases do lead somewhere else, but they are there, you look at them, stair by stair, and follow the details of the bannisters. Perhaps his grey walls *are* hiding something, but one's memory stops short at them, at their cracked plaster, and at their lizards" (*STNN* 159).

Accustomed as one is to the many symbolic and allegorical approaches to Kafka, this *chosiste* approach appears rather eccentric. Of course, there are certain texts by Kafka that attempt to describe things as such, what the Germans call *Dinglichkeit*. Some of the short pieces known as his "enigmas"—"The Cares of a Family Man," "A Visit to a Mine," "Eleven Sons,"[2] and others—can be understood as such, as experiments in pure objectivity.[3] But surely this is no more than a marginal episode in the career of a writer who was definitely less interested in the details of the banisters than in where the staircase leads. Robbe-Grillet's approach to Kafka, though an understandable protest against his allegorizers and a welcome reminder of his "tangible universe" (*STNN* 159), is basically wrong-headed. For it goes one crucial step too far in its reaction against Kafka's theologizers and ontologizers. It throws away the baby with the bathwater—the highly original epistemological status of Kafka's fiction—with its deplorable reduction to a narrow system of thought.

Robbe-Grillet's way of misunderstanding Kafka is the very opposite of Camus's. If Camus denounced the Kafka of *The Castle* (unlike that of *The Trial*) for the wrong reasons, Robbe-Grillet embraces him for the opposite wrong reasons. Camus deplored his (supposed) "leaping" to transcendence; Robbe-Grillet embraces his (supposed) indifference to transcendence. For Camus, Kafka, in *The Castle,* had betrayed the cause of the absurd; for Robbe-Grillet, he should never have been tainted by it: "Are we now dealing with what people call the absurd? Certainly not . . . with the suspicion of absurdity, the metaphysical danger returns" (*STNN* 158).

But is Robbe-Grillet himself entirely free from metaphysical dangers? And is he entirely happy with his own *Verdinglichung* of Kafka? The very fact that he chose staircases and walls to illustrate Kafka's "material world" is significant. For staircases and walls are not self-sufficient objects: staircases "do lead somewhere else," and walls "*are* hiding something." Sartre used precisely the image of "staircases that lead to nothing" to illustrate Kafka's fantastic world, in which material objects rebel against their human ends. Robbe-Grillet now is omitting the end altogether and observing the material staircases only. But he cannot possibly ignore the functionality of staircases, their metonymic status that nilly-willy brings the metaphysical back. His ambivalence shows even more clearly when he defines Kafka the realist as "a creator of a material world *with a visionary presence*" (*STNN* 158; my italics). Surely there is little "visionary presence" in cracked plaster or lizards, as such. A visionary presence comes dangerously near to metaphysics.

II   Robbe-Grillet, in other words, tries to make Kafka conform to his own *chosisme* but gets entangled in a paradox that informs his own work as well.

As Dorrit Cohn has shown, the words that Robbe-Grillet used to reject symbolic interpretations of Kafka's work and to insist on its strict physicality are almost identical with the words he used to reject the symbolic interpretation of his own novel *In The Labyrinth:* "The reality here in question is strictly physical, that is to say it has no allegorical significance. The reader should therefore see in it only the objects, the gestures, the words and the events that are told, without seeking to give them either more or less meaning than they would have in his own life, or in his own death."[4] But in the case of *In The Labyrinth,* too, he seems to have had some doubts about its "strict physicality." "Il y a une part de metaphysique dans ce livre," he admitted to an interviewer.[5]

"Profound metaphysical meanings" (*STNN* 159) thus seem to interfere time and again with Robbe-Grillet's *chosiste* approach to Kafka, as well as with his own *chosisme.* One could claim, moreover, that what gives his novels their nervous energy is precisely the "profound meanings" that keep exploding his "material world" from within. For once a material world is invented, be it Kafka's world of walls and staircases or Robbe-Grillet's own banana plantations and islands, it cannot but betray the mental structure that gave it birth, a mental structure that transcends the banisters or bananas themselves.

The material and the mental, the real and the imagined thus meet and merge. Elsewhere in "From Realism to Reality" Robbe-Grillet speaks of the "mutual dissolution of the two terms" of the dichotomy "imagination-reality" (*STNN* 160). The imagined becomes the real and the real the imagined. For Robbe-Grillet, Kafka's world, as well as his own, is strictly physical and yet has a "visionary presence" because the distinction between physical and visionary, world and mind, objective and subjective no longer holds.

In Kafka the blurring of this distinction is sometimes lent a blatant thematic form. Mind and world encroach upon each other and produce extreme disorientation. Joseph K., for instance, looking for the place of interrogation, invents a joiner by the name of Lanz in order to be able to inquire at the doors whether he lives there and get a chance to look into the rooms. Finally he is actually invited to step in: his invention is "confirmed" by reality (*T* 44–45). Likewise, K. of *The Castle* tells a lie over the telephone, saying he is the old assistant, and the Castle confirms his lie (*C* 26–27). More generally, the confusion between outside world and self-projection is central to many Kafka texts and a major element in his skepticism. One's object of knowledge is always hidden by the shadow one's mind casts.

To what extent is it central also to Robbe-Grillet? *The Voyeur* (1955) includes an episode that seems analogous to the Lanz episode from *The Trial*. It concerns an imaginary "Jean Robin," a name Mathias, the protagonist, invents in order to make friends with the proprietor of a café.[6] Later on, an unknown fisherman comes up to Mathias and greets him as an old friend; his name, written on the door of the cottage he leads him to, is Jean Robin (*Voyeur* 107, 113). Reality, that is, turns a casual figment of the imagination into hard fact. A similar but far more complex example is Mathias's visit (or supposed visit) to the Marek farm.

We first hear of Mathias's plan to get to the farm at the end of part 1 of the novel: "He thought he would make at least an appearance at the Marek farm: he had known the family for so long, certainly he would sell everything there" (*Voyeur* 70–71). But does he carry out his plan, or is he using it only as an alibi to prove his innocence of the girl's murder? When he meets old Madame Marek at the beginning of part 2 (has the murder taken place on the blank page between parts 1 and 2?), he thinks of telling her that he had not gotten to the farm for lack of time and because his rented bicycle was not working properly (*Voyeur* 77–78). He is about to say so when she interrupts him and tells him he wouldn't have found anyone in the house (*Voyeur* 79). Then he tells her he *had* been there and found the house empty (*Voyeur* 79–80). There follows a description (real? imagined?) of the visit (*Voyeur* 80–81), ending with Mathias's disappointment when nobody is found to be at home: "He is very disappointed. Here, at least, he was hoping for a more favorable reception. All the way to the farm his spirits had been rising at the prospect of a visit to his old childhood friends, never suspecting they could all be away from home at once" (*Voyeur* 81). These lines include a reference back to the earlier "free indirect discourse" passage, where Mathias's voice, speaking to Madame Marek, was combined with the narrator's voice: "He hoped for a more favorable reception at the Marek's at least" (*Voyeur* 79). But these lines also anticipate the subsequent description of the same visit: "Ever since that morning—ever since the night before—his spirits had been rising at the prospect of a visit to his old childhood friends" (*Voyeur* 81), a description that also starts as free indirect discourse but gradually leaves Mathias's voice behind and becomes, it seems, univocal, limited to the narrator's voice.

Thus, the above-quoted lines combine bivocality with univocality, making it impossible to distinguish between the character's voice and the narrator's. As a result, Mathias's voice is lent the objective authority of the narrator's, while the latter is lent the uncertain status of the former. The following univocal description of the same visit (*Voyeur* 82–84) abounds, moreover, in verbal echoes of the previous bivocal description of the same (compare *Voyeur* 83–84 with 80–81), and ends—in the circular fashion so common in Robbe-Grillet—with the meeting with Madame Marek (*Voyeur* 84) with which the entire episode began (*Voyeur* 76). The way is open for an endless continuation of the insoluble zigzag of subjective-objective, imagination-reality. As the novel proceeds, a dialectics of yes-no concerning the visit to the Marek farm (was it real? supposed?) goes on and on.[7] The confusion between imagination and reality reaches its peak when Julien, Mme. Marek's grandson, confirms Mathias's supposed visit and reinforces his alibi (*Voyeur* 170–72). As in the Jean Robin episode, or in the Lanz episode in *The Trial*, reality becomes a mirror whose real nature is ever hidden behind the onlooker's inescapable reflection.

III   Thus, the deliberate confusion between reality and imagination in *The Voyeur* is achieved partly through plot, but mainly through voice. In the former, thematic, case, as when "Jean Robin" materializes into a real person, the direct inspiration seems to be Kafka. In the latter, linguistic, case, as in the visit (visit?) to the Mareks, the technique is Robbe-Grillet's own. It consists of the repetition of the same phrases or sentences in passages of free indirect discourse and in passages limited to the narrator's voice, thus giving an ambiguous status to both: what seemed attributable to a character's imagination (though free indirect discourse itself is marked by an indeterminacy of the vocal origin)[8] is lent the objective authority of the narrator's voice, while what seemed to be neutrally reported by the narrator is undermined through verbal analogies with the character's voice.

This technique is symptomatic of Robbe-Grillet's literariness. The repetition of words, phrases, sentences, even entire paragraphs, in the character's voice and in the narrator's, is part of the more general device of repetition in Robbe-Grillet—a device that, along with others, directs the reader's attention to the text as text and promotes its palpability. As a form of what Roman Jakobson calls "the principle of equivalence" operating on "the axis of combination," this device "deepens the fundamental dichotomy of signs and objects" and works against reference and mimesis.[9] "There is no longer the slightest question of verisimilitude," says Robbe-Grillet about the "new realism" (*STNN* 157).

One can give repetition a realistic psychological motivation, of course, and thus make it mimetic. The many repetitions of sea gull, figure eight, exposed nape of girl's neck, or oilcloth with pattern of little flowers in *The Voyeur* have often been interpreted as reflecting sexual obsessiveness. So have the many repetitions in *Jealousy*. But the fact that what is repeated is not just the image but the very words in which it was couched, their grammar and syntax, shows the inadequacy of the mimetic approach. It certainly does not work with the specific type of repetition described above.

Instead, Robbe-Grillet is clearly directing attention to writing as such, to narrative technique as such. The confusion between imagination and reality also engages Robbe-Grillet's mind as a narratological, not epistemological, issue. It has to do with questions such as the relation of narrative fiction to reality, the authority of the narrator, the relation between narrator and character, and so on. The visit to the Marek farm remains suspended between imagination and reality because one is uncertain of the distinction not between mind and world, but between narrator and character. Does Mathias's lie turn into truth when put into the mouth of a supposedly reliable narrator? Does the narrator's truth turn into a lie when put into Mathias's mouth? Why should the very same words like "we hoped for a more favorable reception" be imagination when appearing in a free indirect discourse passage and reality when sponsored by the narrator alone? After all, isn't the narrator equally "quoted" by the author?[10] And what validity does the distinction between imagination and reality have at all in a context that is imaginary in the first place?

The unsolved riddle of the visit to the Marek farm is therefore part of the novel's (and, more generally, the nouveau roman's) reflexivity, its concern with itself as fiction. In what sense can Mathias's imagined act be said to be imagined when embedded in the "false" universe of *The Voyeur*? In what sense can it be discredited by truth in a universe that excludes truth? And, by extension, how can the false world of a novel have a truth value at all, a profound meaning, a thesis? Shouldn't we stick to its gestures and movements, "the only real things," and avoid all questions of application to reality?

What is at stake for Kafka, on the other hand, is much more than writing or the status of fiction. If he too deprives fiction of its truth value or thesis, it is not because fiction is inadequate but because mind is inadequate. That is why the confusion between reality and imagination occurs in Kafka at the level of plot, not of voice. It is a question of the structure of reality, not its narration. When Joseph K. makes up a "Lanz" and then comes across him, the very structure of reality is distorted, a literal metamorphosis of whim into fact takes place. When Mathias seems to be fabricating a visit to the Mareks and then has it confirmed by Julien, only the modes of narrative fiction are questioned: narrator's voice and character's voice can no longer be safely distinguished from one another, particularly since the former keeps secret the one fact that really counts.

IV   An analysis of the techniques Robbe-Grillet uses in other novels to abolish the distinction between real and imagined will confirm this. Robbe-Grillet, when compared to Kafka, is clearly interested in writing rather than world, in medium rather than message.

In *Jealousy* (1957), which has no grammatically defined speaker, it is a question of perspective rather than voice, focalization rather than narration. This best known of Robbe-Grillet's novels has been a popular bone of contention between *chosistes* and psychologists, for it abounds in the minutest "objectal" descriptions but also provides the most nonobjective motivation for them all: the narrator's obsessive jealousy. That the conflict between strict physicality and "profound meaning" is deliberate shows in the word Robbe-Grillet chose as title: "jalousie" in French means both "jealousy" and "venetian blind."

Those who believe the novel to be a study in obsessive jealousy subsume all those endless objective descriptions under this obsession. Not only A.'s lustrous hair, an obvious object for desire, but the rows of banana trees, their numbers and angles, have been subjected to jealousy, their seeming objectivity explained as a tortured soul's escape from obsessive emotion to the calm neutrality of nature. I wonder, however, whether the close juxtaposition of madly jealous eye and coolly measuring intellect is psychologically credible: "A.'s arms, a little less distinct than her neighbor's because of the color—though light—of the material of her dress, are also lying on the elbow-rests of her chair. The four hands are lying in a row, motionless. The space between A.'s left hand and Franck's right hand is approximately two inches."[11] Or when the seeing eye follows A.'s head, arms, and upper body as they disappear in the window of Franck's car, obscuring what is happening inside, almost a "primal scene" in the jealousy and curiosity it arouses—and a few lines later, when A. is back in front of the door of the house: "From this point she sees the whole house down the middle: the main room (living room on the left and dining room on the right, where the table is already set for dinner), the central hallway (off which open five doors, all closed, three on the right and two on the left),"[12] and so on. It is hardly a single perspective that can be so overwhelmed by emotion and at the same time count doors and scrupulously indicate directions.

It therefore seems that there are *two* perspectives at work here and that they exist side by side in this novel. The one perhaps an external narrator's, is strictly *chosiste,* constructing an extremely detailed material setting: a house, its veranda, living room, bedrooms, courtyard, banana trees surrounding it. The other, the jealous husband's, is obsessively projective, seeing the constructed setting exclusively in terms of desire, though never mentioning its terms, perhaps unaware of them. The inability to tell projection from reality and reality from projection is brought out here through blurred transitions from one focus to another rather than from one voice to another, as in *The Voyeur.* The problem is not Who speaks? but Who sees?; not Is it the narrator or the character who says this? but Is it the naked eye or desire that sees this? In either case narrative fiction, dissolving its reality into imagination and vice versa, can no longer guide us from an imagined world to a truth.

A third way of blurring between the real and the imagined can be found in *In the Labyrinth,* which was also third in order of publication (1959). Here it is a question of neither voice nor focus but of narrative levels.[13] Items that belong to a story within a story come out of their story and enter the larger story, and vice versa.

Following all the oscillations between the narrative levels that make up this novel would be a long and tiresome task. Let me only refer to the most obvious case. The engraving that hangs on the wall of the room with which the novel opens, a café scene after a military disaster, with the caption "The Defeat at Reichenfels" (*Labyrinth* 22), turns into narrative (*Labyrinth* 24) and becomes one with the story itself. There are enough parallels, or rather identifications, between elements of the engraving and those of life outside it (notably the parcel containing the belongings of the dead comrade, which the soldier protagonist is supposed to give to the dead man's father), to blur the distinction between picture and reality. Reality becomes as fictitious as a picture, while the picture, encroaching upon reality, becomes no less real than reality. The room with which the novel opens and ends is populated with elements of both the story and the story within the story, both the engraving itself and the parcel from the story told in the engraving. It is a tangled hierarchy, abounding in "strange loops."[14]

V The sheer technical brilliance with which the three devices—mixed voices, mixed foci, mixed narrative levels—are executed must necessarily direct attention to itself. The clever manip-
ulation of the conventions of the novel is bound to engage the
reader's mind to the exclusion of all extraliterary matters. All three
novels are about novel writing. Robbe-Grillet's own comment on
The Erasers and *The Voyeur* applies to all three: "N'est ce pas simple-
ment que le mouvement de l'ecriture y est plus important que celui
des passions et des crimes?"[15]

Passions and crimes are not important to Kafka either. But
neither is novel writing. Or rather, neither are questions such as
voice, focus, or narrative level, except as directly relevant to meaning. One could, of course, find in Kafka analogous techniques to
those we have seen in *Jealousy* and *In the Labyrinth*. The mixture of
foci in *Jealousy* may be said to underlie all those cases in Kafka
where the distinction is blurred between outside world and self-
projection. The mixture of narrative levels in *In the Labyrinth* also
underlies those episodes in Kafka, like the Bürgel episode, where
quoted message and its context are presented as parallel to such an
extent that they become identical. In the end, however, Kafka's
total vision, which supersedes psychology and ethics and politics in
its metaphysical stride, cannot be distracted by narratology. There
can be little difference between narrator's voice and character's
voice in a universe in which all voices are doomed to ignorance.
There can be no question of objective versus projective perspective
where all eyes are blind.

That is why Kafka's writing strikes us as so utterly unobtrusive
and utterly unforegrounded, except perhaps in its deliberate cor-
rectness. It is wholly transparent, hardly ever drawing attention to
itself, only to the fantastic material world it creates. This is a world
forceful enough to be irreducible and yet to have the visionary
presence of the inexplicable.

5

The Ladder Kicked Away: Beckett and Kafka

His was always a story with a hole in it: a wrong story, always wrong.
—*J. M. Coetzee,* Life & Times of Michael K

▌ In an article published in 1961 Ruby Cohn drew a comparison between Beckett's *Watt* and Kafka's *The Castle*, the only work by Kafka that Beckett claimed to have read seriously and in the original.[1] This comparison has often been endorsed since. The heroes of both novels, says Cohn, move through an absurd universe in a compulsive quest that they never understand. They both desire to see an enigmatic, perhaps godlike, ever-changing figure—the Count in *The Castle*, Mr. Knott in *Watt,* and though K. never gets to the Castle, while Watt enters Mr. Knott's house and joins his household, they fail equally. "In both novels," says Cohn, "the failure of the quest results from the human limitation of the hero. In both novels, mystic forces prove impregnable to weak human siege, and indifferently continue to be."

That Mr. Knott *is* a mystic force impregnable to human siege—a siege of minds rather than swords, as Cohn puts it—is manifest enough. Beckett goes out of his way to underline Knott's divine symbolism. Mr. Knott's house, for instance, "as it was now, so it had been in the beginning, and so it would remain to the end."[2] Knott himself, at the same time, is "seldom the same figure," he is fantastically "various" (*W* 146); there is no place where he is not (*W* 198–99); he needs nothing—except "one, not to need, and two, a witness to his not needing" (*W* 202). As for his transcendence to mind, Watt, though he enters the house and works there, has no conception of him (*W* 118), knows nothing of him (W 147), remains in particular ignorance of his nature (*W* 199), abandons all hopes of ever seeing him face-to-face (*W* 145). The few glimpses he catches of him are caught, as it were, in a glass (*W* 146), and, in explicit theological terms, any speculation about the reasons for Mr. Knott's grotesquely unsuitable clothing is "an anthropomorphic insolence of short duration" (*W* 202).

His clothing, however, *is* grotesque, and it is described at grotesque length. It must suffice to mention that he can be barefoot and dressed for boating when it snows, or wrapped in furs in summer by his fire (*W* 202). His infinite variety reminds Ruby Cohn, as well as later critics,[3] of Klamm of *The Castle*. Klamm too is both unapproachable and ever fluctuating, both one and various (*C* 167). But—and this is the main point I should like to make about Beckett's relation to Kafka in *Watt*—the tension between transcendence and verbalization in Beckett becomes such that the very possibility of narration is put in question. The irretrievable loss of the *Halakhah,* which in Kafka had not destroyed *Aggadah* but had given it its paradoxical status of simultaneous autonomy and dependence, here affects *Aggadah* itself. Beckett is hopelessly caught in the web of story telling itself and, consequently, of obsessive reflexivity. Kafka's ability, at his best and most heroic, to overcome fragmentariness and mold what Benjamin calls the "relics" of the lost doctrine into full-blown myths—his ability to "cling to the transmissibility of truth" even while losing truth itself—is not given to Beckett. Meaninglessness to Beckett spells nothingness, and the narrative intended to transmit nothingness necessarily disintegrates into an obsessive concern with itself. Thus, Beckett may be said to carry out a potential in Kafka that Kafka himself was determined to avoid, though not without the desperate struggle to which his diaries and notebooks give ample evidence.

II   To see how Beckett does this, let us first go back to what *Watt* shares not only with *The Castle,* but with Kafka as a whole. For not only *The Castle* but also *The Trial* and "The Metamorphosis" can be regarded as failed bildungsromane—or rather as stories about failed *Bildung*— and in this *Watt* strongly resembles them.

K., Joseph K., and Gregor Samsa all think humanly, that is, in more or less rational terms. They all experience a traumatic, inconceivable event (metamorphosis, arrest for nothing) and/or hear a crucial lesson (the priest's words in the cathedral, Bürgel's words to K.) that should teach them to change their ways of thinking. But their *Bildung* fails. Samsa dies thinking vacant (though peaceful) thoughts: he has not understood much of what has happened. Joseph K., notwithstanding the priest's words, still looks for "some arguments in his favor," as the butcher's knife is already at his throat. And K. of *The Castle* sleeps through Bürgel's message of salvation.

K.'s sleep is no accident, of course. If he falls asleep it is, as Bürgel tells him, because "one's physical energies last only to a certain limit. Who can help the fact that precisely this limit is significant in other ways too?" (*C* 254). Our powers, that is, are strictly limited, and they reach precisely to the point where salvation begins. Sleep or fatigue—human consciousness's declared limit—is the typical response of Kafka's heroes in the face of the inexplicable. Thus Joseph K., as we have seen, is too tired to follow when the priest, summing up his long exegesis of the parable "Before the Law," tells him he must replace thinking in terms of truth by thinking in terms of necessity (*T* 243).[4] And thus K. is ironically sinking further and further in sleep while Bürgel is telling him at last how to get to the Castle (*C* 243–55).

Interestingly, Watt, like the two K.s, is subjected to a long speech and reacts similarly. Arsene, his predecessor in Mr. Knott's household, subjects him to a "short statement" (*W* 37) that lasts for twenty-five pages, which Watt receives with a combination of physical awareness and mental fatigue reminiscent of K.'s reaction to Bürgel's words: "He wondered what Arsene had meant, nay, he wondered what Arsene had said, on the evening of his departure. For his declaration had entered Watt's ears only by fits, and his understanding, like all that enters the ear only by fits, hardly at all. He had realized, to be sure, that Arsene was speaking and in a sense to him, but something had prevented him, perhaps his fatigue, from paying attention to what was being said and from enquiring into what was being meant" (*W* 77). It is Watt's fatigue that prevents him from paying attention. Perhaps this is why he learns as little from Arsene's words as Joseph K. learns from the priest's or K. from Bürgel's. Above all, Arsene's words about "the unutterable or ineffable" (*W* 61), important though rather casual and lost under a mountain of verbiage, seem totally wasted on him: he goes on "desir[ing] words to be applied" to everything (*W* 78).

Elsewhere, too, fatigue seems typical of Watt no less than of the two K.s. It is "mere fatigue" that may explain why he no longer wishes—or fears—to see Mr. Knott face-to-face (*W* 145–46). And, on finally leaving Knott's house, his fatigue when standing in the kitchen with his two bags is so great that he is on the verge of falling into an "uneasy sleep" (*W* 220–21). Appropriately, the long stay at Mr. Knott's house, which had led to hardly any knowledge at all, must end in a final, devastating fatigue.

But is Arsene's monologue modeled on Bürgel's—or on the priest's—beyond the fact that it sends its listener to sleep, and that sleep, as in Kafka, seems to stand for the limitation of mind? Is Arsene trying to give Watt some *Bildung,* and does this *Bildung* resemble Bürgel's, or perhaps the priest's?

In the long speech that K. misses by falling asleep, Bürgel tells him that to get to the Castle the applicant must come unannounced in the middle of the night to the room of an incompetent secretary. But this "message," as we have seen, is a mere mirror image of what is actually happening: K. *has* come unannounced in the middle of the night to the room of an incompetent secretary. Bürgel, thus, is merely offering K. a mirror.

It also turns out that Bürgel—or the Castle—is as eagerly awaiting K. as K. is awaiting him. The applicant is always expected by the secretary, "truly thirstingly expected and always reasonably regarded as out of reach" (*C* 252). It seems, furthermore, that all the other figures connected with the Castle—Barnabas, Olga, Hans, Gardena—need K. as much as he needs them. Those whom he regards as means to his end regard him as the means to their own ends.[5]

The reduction of all messages from, and means of access to the Castle to mere mirror images of the quester is one of the techniques Kafka employs to frustrate all hope of knowledge. All that one can hope to know is a reflection of oneself. The long-awaited (and now missed-by-sleep) way to salvation is, ironically, any given moment; it is everywhere and nowhere.

A close reading of the first few pages of Arsene's "statement" will show that Beckett is using a similar technique to that used in the Bürgel episode.[6] Arsene's own arrival comes back to him when he sees the newly arrived Watt, and he describes his arrival in terms that repeat the actual description of Watt's arrival a few pages earlier. Some of the words repeated are "dark," "red," "paths," "grass," "birds," "little sounds," "coming and going."[7] He "has arrived," says Arsene, "he even ventures to remove his hat, and set down his bags" (*W* 39)—and Watt, three pages earlier, "set down his bags . . . took off his hat, for he had reached his destination" (*W* 36).

As in *The Castle*, this device is only one thread in a web of mirror images that extends throughout the novel and enlarges Watt's perplexity to include the reader himself: Who is Knott? Who is Watt? Who is the seeker? Who is sought? For in the same way as the representatives of the Castle turn out to be in search of K. no less than he is in search of them, Knott, too, seems to need Watt. We have already seen his description, needing nothing except "a witness to his not needing" (*W* 202). In Arsene's speech the master's existence is said to depend on the existence of his parlor maids as their existence depends on him (*W* 49). And in the incoherent words that Watt says to Sam, the narrator, in the asylum—with word order, letter order, and sentence order all inverted—he presents himself and Knott as two equals, a typical Beckettesque pair of bums. This is how Raymond Federman, in his book on Beckett's early fiction, reorganizes Watt's muddled speech: "Sid by sid, two min. Al day, part of nit. Dum, num, blind. Knot look at wat? No. Wat look at knot? No. Wat talk to knot? No. Knot talk to wat? No. Wat den did us do? Niks, niks, niks, part of nit, al day. Two men, sid by sid."[8] And at the end of the novel, as Federman points out, Knott is wearing a single boot, just as in the beginning Watt was described as having one foot bare.[9] Obversely, Watt shares Knott's divine attributes—his variety,[10] his transcendence to mind,[11] and, as the narrator notes, his resemblance to Christ (*W* 157). No wonder the names Watt and Knott become almost interchangeable.[12]

At other times Watt becomes a reflection of the narrator (*W* 157), further thickening the novel's texture of coalescences. As in *The Castle*, the very purpose and direction of the quest is upset by the blurring of the distinction between quester and object.

III   This mirroring rather than informative quality is one element that Arsene's speech shares with Bürgel's. His speech can hardly be informative, for "what we know," he says, "partakes in no small measure of the nature of what has so happily been called the unutterable or ineffable, so that any attempt to utter or eff it is doomed to fail, doomed, doomed to fail" (*W* 61).

Nonetheless, Arsene tries to "eff" it. He describes a sort of mystical experience at whose center there is a change. This change can be "effed" only by means of a tautology ("What was changed . . . was the sentiment that a change . . . had taken place," *W 42)*, or a paradox ("that presence of what did not exist," *W* 43). But Arsene seems unhappy with such meager formulas. His more typical "effing" is a compulsive piling up of redundant words and sentences: "For Vincent and Walter were not the first, ho no, but before them were Vincent and another whose name I forget, and before them that other whose name I forget, and another whose name I also forget . . . and before them that other whose name I never knew and another whose name Walter could not recall, and before them that other whose name Walter could not recall" (*W* 58), and so on and so on. The use of language here only serves to set off the inadequacy of language, for it appears here in its most blatantly futile form. To list Knott's servants, as Arsene does, by specifying those who forgot their names, is to emit hot air. It is as absurd as defining birds by specifying which type of butterfly they are not.

This is language used no longer, as in Kafka, to point to "a reverse side to the décor," to suggest "an inhuman, undecipherable order."[13] It is rather language used to *replace* the décor, which has collapsed with the loss of its "reverse side." Arsene, or any Beckett-esque narrator for that matter, forgets his narrative, or cannot recall it, or never knew it. He is inescapably caught in the web of his forgetting. It is narrative reduced to a tantrum about its own impossibility.

The tension between nothingness and the compulsive compilation of words marks Arsene's monologue. This tension is ironically enacted in the amusing gap between the description of the monologue as a "short statement" and the actual twenty-five pages it occupies. Not only Arsene's speech but the entire novel bristles with those absurd series, the mechanical—partly hilarious, partly infuriating—enumeration of all logical possibilities implied in a certain configuration. This "comedy of exhaustive enumeration," to use Beckett's own description of vaudeville,[14] can be said, indeed, to be the trademark of this novel. Its juxtaposition with the lyrical passages and their often Joycean syntactic modulations creates a highly moving counterpoint peculiar to *Watt*.

But isn't this a far cry from Kafka, and from Bürgel or the priest, to whose speeches we have been comparing Arsene's? There is neither lyricism nor exhaustive enumeration in Kafka. His language is hardly foregrounded at all. Kafka counts on his narrative to do the job and needs no linguistic fireworks to replace it.

The radical foregrounding of language in Beckett, as against its remarkable backgrounding in Kafka, has to do with the collapse of narrative in the former. Once the transmissibility of truth, not only truth itself, becomes a problem, its medium—language—loses its transparency and grows opaque and obsessively intrusive. It now occupies the entire stage, hiding whatever it was supposed to reveal. The separation of man from truth now shows in the breakdown of the medium, the aberrations of speech. It is no accident that Arsene should speak of the "unutterable or ineffable," while Kafka, for whom the problem lies not in the medium itself but in its relation to meaning, prefers the "inexplicable" or "incomprehensible."[15]

If Arsene and, more generally, Watt weave an intricate web of utterances around the unutterable, Kafka weaves a web of explanations around the inexplicable. Both overdo it to undo it. Like Arsene's overlong "short statement," the priest's hair-splitting commentary on the parable "Before the Law" is made only to be unmade. "The Scriptures are unalterable, and the comments often enough merely express the commentator's despair." This strategy—explanations offered only to be withdrawn, action taken only to be taken back—is, we have seen, Kafka's way of deconstructing his own meanings.

IV In the less obsessive pages of *Watt* Beckett uses devices that are more directly Kafkaesque in that they convey uncertainty flatly and without slipping into the nervous tic of "exhaustive enumeration." Such is the oscillation between "yes" and "no" regarding the assertion that Watt would come down the stairs and up again once a day (*W* 116). As in Bürgel's oscillation with regard to the possibility of exploiting the "nocturnal weakness" of the secretaries (*C* 249), the successive sentences here enact a similar inability to opt for one alternative. Little words such as "not so," "unless," "but," "and yet" proliferate, as in Kafka. Elsewhere, a series of "perhapses" is offered without a final decision,[16] or a passage that begins in certainty ends in doubt,[17] or a statement is negated in a parenthetical clause, then carried on regardless of the negating clause.[18] These are all typical Kafkaesque techniques, imitating the flat modulations of "correct" discourse.

More often, however, Watt may be said to take literally what Olga, in *The Castle,* says about the letters from the Castle: "The reflections they give rise to are endless, and chance determines where one stops reflecting" (*C* 216). But Olga does not enumerate those endless reflections. In Kafka endless reflection is only implicit in things, the basis for the irresolvable ambiguity and indecision that fill his world, but it does not disrupt his narrative in the stories he completed. Endless indecision lurks everywhere but is vanquished by the writer's mythopoeic drive. In *Watt* endless reflection breaks loose, becomes wildly explicit—becomes both comic and pathological. The comedy and the pathology thicken the novel's texture, neuroticize it, bring it closest to that type of neurotic style called the obsessive-compulsive and marked by extreme rigidity of thinking and the loss of reality.[19] This rigidity insists on logical completion and compels Watt to spend pages in exhausting, for example, every possible combination of sock, stocking, boot, shoe, and slipper on each of Knott's feet (*W* 200–201). But logical completion, in the thinking of a compulsive "living machine,"[20] leads to irrationality, to loss of reality. Wilhelm Reich says about this character that "there is a marked inability to focus attention on what is rationally important about an object and to disregard its superficial aspects. Attention is evenly distributed; questions of secondary importance are accorded the same thoroughness as those at the center of professional interests. The more pathological and rigid this trait is, the more attention is concentrated on things of secondary importance and the rationally more important matters are sidetracked."[21]

That is exactly what Watt keeps doing. His attention is concentrated on trivia, while what really matters remains untouched and obscure. Furthermore, and this is where the comedy mainly lies, what *is* touched is mechanically presented in all its combinations regardless of whether the components are at all combinable. Thus, for instance, the three components of Mr. Knott's attitude to the arrangement concerning his meals are: (1) Mr. Knott was responsible for the arrangement; (2) he knew he was responsible for the arrangement; and (3) he was content. The three components, affirmed and negated, are combined into twelve possibilities, some of which are hilariously impossible, but presumably "worthy of serious consideration." For example: "(11) Mr. Knott was responsible for the arrangement, but knew who was responsible for the arrangement, but did not know that any such arrangement existed, and was content; (12) Mr. Knott was not responsible for the arrangement, but knew that he was responsible for the arrangement, but did not know that any such arrangement existed, and was content" (*W* 87). This, of course, is no longer obsessive logicality. It is gross illogicality. The living machine carries on regardless of the fact that it has not been fed with some indispensable logical rules. Its neurotic style perfectly serves Beckett's aim to combine an endless proliferation of words with an endless dwindling of meaning.

Kafka, on the other hand, seldom digresses from normal thinking. The gap between the pedestrian mind and the world is wide enough for him; no obsessive-compulsive style of thinking is needed to demonstrate it. When a man finds himself transformed in his bed into an insect, the rather unimaginative conclusion that "this getting up early makes one quite stupid" (*CS* 90) is inadequate enough, comic enough. And so are Joseph K.'s sensible words after being arrested: "If I had behaved sensibly, nothing further would have happened" (*T* 27). Kafka derives his most powerful effects from such "normal" responses to the abnormal that invades his fictional world. This is perhaps what Beckett means when he says that the Kafka hero is "lost but he's not spiritually precarious, he's not falling to bits."[22] If his own people, as he adds, *are* falling to bits, that is because they can no longer function in a coherent fictional world and have neurotically replaced it with language.

Their indecisiveness—another obsessive-compulsive trait[23]—is pathetic; Arsene knows "by the look" of Watt that he will leave everything undecided (*W* 43). Also pathetic is their anxiety lest they be misunderstood and their thoroughness be proven incomplete. Watt is inwardly cruelly coerced to remind his listener over and over again that he knows he is talking only about what he is talking about, lest they assume he doesn't know that there are other things he could talk about:

> and sometimes they sang and cried and stated and murmured, all together, at the same time, as now, to mention only these four kinds of voices, for there were others. (*W* 27)
>
> like an oak, an elm, a beech or an ash, to mention only the oak, the elm, the beech and the ash. (*W* 56)
>
> For the chairs also, to mention only the chairs also. . . . For the corners also, to mention only the corners also. (*W* 206–7)
>
> For daily changed, as well as these, in carriage, expression, shape and size, the feet, the legs, the hands, the arms, the mouth, the nose, the eyes, the ears, to mention only the feet, the legs, the hands, the arms, the mouth, the nose, the eyes, the ears, and their carriage, expression, shape and size. (*W* 211)

This comedy of anxiety, both harrowing and ludicrous, is all Beckett's own. In the final analysis, however, it is the mere unfolding of an anxiety that informs Kafka's whole work, though it seldom becomes explicit there. One of the rare places where it almost does is the early short piece "On the Tram":

> I stand on the end platform of the tram and am completely unsure of my footing in this world, in this town, in my family. Not even casually could I indicate any claims that I might rightly advance in any direction. I have not even any defense to offer for standing on this platform, holding on to this strap, letting myself be carried along by this tram, nor for the people who give way to the tram or walk quietly along or stand gazing into shopwindows. Nobody asks me to put up a defense indeed, but that is irrelevant.[24] (*CS* 388–89)

First it seems that it is only his own life that the speaker feels obliged to defend, which would be easy to explain in psychological terms. But then it turns out that he must also offer defenses for people in the street, those walking along and those looking at shop windows. He must, that is, offer an apologia for any fact, for the cruel rule of *determinatio negatio est,* according to which one cannot establish a fact without negating all other alternatives, one cannot assert p without rejecting non-p.[25] The anxiety and guilt to which this iron rule gives rise, a fear of opting for the wrong alternative and proving a liar, is one epistemological explanation for Kafka's lifelong reluctance to impose completed narrative patterns on reality, and the resulting fragmentariness of so many of his texts, as well as their effect—even when completed—of stationary running or perpetual zigzag. In Beckett's *Watt* this fear becomes painfully explicit in those endless "to mention only"s, a compulsive apologia for the necessary limitation even of his seemingly unlimited speech. If we could only mention everything, we might be saved. That is what Watt calls "semantic succour" (*W* 79).

V　　The need for semantic succour hardly exists in Kafka. It appears in the early "Description of a Struggle," where the Supplicant "pelts" things with "any old names" (*CS* 33) to control their threat, just as Watt will "set to trying names on things, and on himself, almost as a woman hats" (*W* 80). Kafka's Supplicant calls the poplar "Tower of Babel" or "Noah in his cups" (*CS* 33), while Beckett's Watt calls the pot "shield" and "raven" (*W* 80). Later on, however, Kafka hardly comes back to what must have struck him by then as irrelevant to his true concern. The succour that Samsa and K. need is far beyond semantics.

Watt, on the other hand, needs semantic succour because old words, a pillow for his head (*W* 115), abandon their signifieds and leave them indeterminable, unnarratable, dangerous. The piano tuners' visit gradually loses "all meaning, even the most literal" (*W* 69), and the pot "for Watt alone [is] not a pot any more" (*W* 79). The problem, thus, is located *before* verbalization, not after it; it is the problem of how to *achieve* a story, not how to interpret it. In Kafka it was the symbolic meaning of the literal that was lost; in Beckett it is the literal itself. To go back to Sartre's image, the décor itself, not only its reverse side, has toppled; or, to use Arsene's image, the ladder has been taken away and one can no longer come down it (*W* 42).

The emptiness that now fills the stage cannot be said to be incomprehensible, for it is nothing. Only something can be incomprehensible. Kafka's incomprehensible is "something unknown to us" (*CS* 457). The "ineffable" in *Watt* is "a nothing" (*W* 77). To say of Kafka's Castle that it stands for nothing would make it comprehensible. It would be as reductive as saying that it stands for grace. In deconstructing all symbolic meaning Kafka also deconstructs the nihilistic one.

In *Watt*, on the other hand, the disintegration of narrative leaves nothing. If the piano tuners' visit loses "all meaning, even the most literal," nothing is left to understand or to not understand. That is why phrases denoting meaninglessness are here used interchangeably with phrases denoting nothingness: "where no meaning appeared" (*W* 74), or "events that resisted all Watt's efforts to saddle them with meaning" (*W* 75), are implicitly equated with "nothing had happened," "a thing that was nothing had happened" (*W* 73), "a nothing had happened" (*W* 77). What has no meaning is not. To Kafka, what has no meaning is the very core of what is.

6

**Chairs and Legends: Ionesco
and Kafka**

I   Before one can see how Ionesco relates to Kafka, one must
first note, of course, that he is a playwright and that Kafka was not.
Kafka *did* try to write a play[1] and had great admiration for the
theater.[2] If nevertheless he preferred writing fiction, that was because his vision called for techniques that only fiction could provide.

A letter he wrote in 1915 to his publisher, Kurt Wolff, may
clarify this point. The letter is not about the theater but about the
possibility that the illustrator Ottomar Starke would do a drawing
for the title page of "The Metamorphosis." Kafka reacts to this
news with near panic:

> This prospect has given me a minor and perhaps unnecessary
> fright. It struck me that Starke, as an illustrator, might want to
> draw the insect itself. Not that, please not that! I do not want
> to restrict him, but only to make this plea out of my deeper
> knowledge of the story. The insect itself cannot be depicted. It
> cannot even be shown from a distance. . . . I would be very
> grateful if you would pass along my request and make it more
> emphatic. If I were to offer suggestions for an illustration, I
> would choose such scenes as the following: the parents and the
> head clerk in front of the locked door, or even better, the par-
> ents and the sister in the lighted room, with the door open
> unto the adjoining room that lies in darkness.[3]

Why is Kafka so concerned? After all, he himself, in his story, depicts the insect in great detail—his domelike brown belly divided
into stiff, arched segments, his numerous thin legs with their sticky

soles, the brown fluid that issues from his mouth. Why shouldn't the illustrator do the same? And as for the perspective he is recommending—that of Samsa's family in front of his door—isn't it a perspective that he himself largely neglects in the story, mostly limiting himself to the insect's point of view, though adding the narrator's whenever Samsa's animality transcends his own self-image?[4]

Kafka's plea, thus, is less than obvious. In the story he depicts the insect and avoids the family's point of view; in the letter he does not want the insect to be depicted and recommends the family's point of view. How is one to explain the contradiction?

Apparently Kafka thought the insect could be described in a story but not in a drawing. Why so? Precisely because a story could both describe the metamorphosed man from the outside and center on his own point of view. The proposed drawing, if it were to depict the insect itself, would have had, on the other hand, to adopt another's perspective. It would thus have worked against Kafka's radical innovation.

The innovation, to put it in Genette's terms, is that the focalizer is the focalized and yet can perceive himself only from the outside.[5] To put it in plain English, the story enters its hero's consciousness but has no access to his inner life. It thus becomes a kind of behavioristic autobiography in the third person. The reader is deprived of the old omniscience and is largely restricted, as in the psychological novel, to a single, partial perspective, but he does not enjoy the psychological novel's insight into the subtleties of feeling and thought. The interior perspective lets him see only the outer manifestations of its owner's thoughts and feelings.

This twofold leanness, dictated by extreme agnosticism, was Kafka's innovation, and he knew that no drawing could do it justice. That is, I think, why he was so insistent that the insect should not be drawn. That may also partly explain why he did not write for the theater. For, although the theater can depict things from the outside and forgo psychology, it has no means of restricting the view to a single perspective and reducing to a minimum other perspectives that would rectify it. Thus, the deep anguish of uncertainty that a Kafka reader shares with his heroes could not be reproduced on the stage. If stage adaptations of Kafka stories strike one as feeble, that is because one has necessarily been released, as viewer, from the stifling perspective of the hero's own eyes. Paradoxically, one has thereby been released from the hero's natural acceptance of the fantastic. One is no longer included in the fantasy; one begins to be amazed. This is a sure sign that one has abandoned the Kafkaesque perspective, that one has come out of the fantastic world and is now viewing it as an outsider, scandalized rather than horrified.

II   The Samsa family facing, as suggested in Kafka's letter, a door wide open, gaping black, cannot but remind one of Amédée Buccinioni and his wife Madeleine facing the half-open door in Ionesco's *Amédée or How to Get Rid of It*. It is not their son-turned-insect hiding behind the door, but a mysterious corpse. But the corpse may in a sense be said to be their dead son, for it is perhaps the corpse of a baby they were once supposed to look after,[6] and being dead it must be gotten rid of, like Samsa at the end of "The Metamorphosis." But while Samsa is very easily gotten rid of—the maid does it with a broom—the corpse, growing up and up until it fills the stage, is a real bother. Unlike Samsa, he will not let the family chase him back to his room to rot quietly there. He must be awkwardly carried out to the street, is then wound round Amédée's waist, and finally opens up like a huge parachute and carries him up to the sky. "Amédée, Amédée," Madeleine cries, "you'll make yourself ill, you haven't taken your mackintosh . . . " (*A* 76). She reacts in the same grotesquely inadequate way that marks Samsa's and his family's reaction to his metamorphosis. They, too, facing an existential upheaval, think in terms of a possible cold.

This Kafkaesque reduction of the fantastic to the commonplace is what Ionesco is after. To achieve it he must not let his characters be surprised by the fantastic. When the corpse's two enormous feet slide slowly in through the open door, Madeleine's cry, the stage directions tell us, should convey fear—"but above all irritation." This, the stage directions go on, "is an embarrassing situation, but it should not seem at all unusual, and the actors should play this scene quite naturally. It is a 'nasty blow' of course, an extremely 'nasty blow,' but no worse than that" (*A* 28). And the American soldier, meeting Amédée in the street and "noticing" the body he is carrying, whose legs alone now fill half the stage, asks "without astonishment, as naturally as possible," whether this is a friend of his (*A* 68).

This emphatic lack of astonishment vis-à-vis the supernatural has for its obverse counterpart an astonishment vis-à-vis the banal. This latter motif, only slightly touched by Kafka,[7] is central to Ionesco's sense of the comic. A classic case in point is *The Bald Soprano*, of which Ionesco has said:

> It was by plunging into banality, by draining the sense from the hollowest clichés of everyday language that I tried to render the strangeness that seems to pervade our whole existence. The tragic and the farcical, the prosaic and the poetic, the realistic and the fantastic, the strange and the ordinary, perhaps these are the contradictory principles (there is no theater without conflict) that may serve as a basis for a new dramatic structure. In this way perhaps the unnatural can by its very violence appear natural and the too natural will avoid the naturalistic.[8]

One notes how smoothly Ionesco passes from the strangeness of the banal to the naturalness of the unnatural; they are two sides of the same coin. The man sitting in the underground reading his newspaper is "extraordinary";[9] the growing corpse is "not at all unusual."

To let the fantastic and the commonplace interpenetrate, to embed the fantastic in the commonplace and the commonplace in the fantastic—this is a central concern of Ionesco's. It is the "flat of a petit bourgeois couple" (*NCN* 26) in which the corpse is growing; it is "completely realistic" furniture[10] that, in *The New Tenant*, fills the town, brings the traffic to a standstill and dams up the Thames. I wonder, however, whether the final effect of this technique is the one described by J. S. Doubrovsky:

> What keeps [Ionesco's] plays from being mere rantings and ravings is the very weight and denseness of their reality, one might almost say their realism. For, as far as we are concerned,

we refuse to consider those literary works as "dreamlike" (*oniriques*) or "surrealistic." That would mean forgetting the meticulous care with which the playwright stresses, without omitting a single one of them, all the details of his deliberately familiar settings. . . . What must be wrenched off its moorings, after the fashion of Rimbaud's Bateau Ivre, what must overturn and capsize is *reality* itself, for, according to the very words of the Architect in *The Unrewarded Killer,* "reality, contrary to dream, can turn into a nightmare." If Ionesco's theater is viewed as compounded of "the stuff dreams are made on," it will lose all its force and be neutralized.[11]

Although I agree that the plays are not dreamlike, I doubt that they would lose their force by being dreamlike and, further, that their not being dreamlike is a result of the meticulous realism of their settings. I think, on the contrary, that a realistic setting is bound to enhance—indeed, is a necessary condition for—the dreamlike effect of the fantastic. "Nothing," to quote Alain Robbe-Grillet, "is more fantastic than precision."[12] I also think that a dreamlike effect, if achieved, would increase, not neutralize, the force of the plays. That it is not achieved is a necessary result of the limitations of the stage.

Take Kafka. Samsa's room and its furniture are as meticulously realistic as Ionesco's petit bourgeois drawing rooms. So are the corridors and offices of *The Trial.* Does this diminish the fantastic effect of what takes place against these settings? To say so would be like saying that the naturalistically rendered stone of a Magritte stone bird makes it less fantastic, less dreamlike. But this dreamlike effect is precisely what Kafka wants because fantasy is real to the dreaming mind only. The waking mind is surprised by it, cannot suspend its own disbelief. Only the dreamer accepts it as truth. A dreamlike effect would only enhance the reality of the growing corpse, of the infinitely proliferating furniture. If Ionesco cannot achieve it notwithstanding his realistic detail, that is because drama cannot have a single, dreaming—that is nonsurprised—perspective. What must be absolutely real to Ionesco's characters cannot be so to his audience. They do not see it with Amédée's or the Tenant's eyes. They awake and—unlike Adam—do not find it truth. This major difference between the experience of a Kafka reader and that of an Ionesco spectator must be kept in mind throughout the following discussion.

III   It is not by accident that what we have said up to now has centered on "The Metamorphosis." To Ionesco, who once made fun of alleged "proofs" that he had been influenced by Kafka (*NCN* 89) but later selected him as the only real influence,[13] "The Metamorphosis" seems to be the very essence of Kafka. He once said that this was the first Kafka story he had read, and that what struck him most about it was "the fact that anyone can become a monster, that it's possible for all of us to become monsters."[14] This glaring example of creative misreading—Ionesco is aware that "this was perhaps not what Kafka wanted his story to show me"[15]—produced *Rhinoceros,* a study of collective metamorphosis, of the dehumanization of a whole community.[16] A metamorphosis into animal marks the ending of *Jack or the Submission* as well.[17]

But above and beyond this obvious misinterpretation (Samsa can be forced into many roles, but hardly into that of a totalitarian conformist), Kafka is important to Ionesco in ways that transcend politics. An example is the embedding we have seen of the surreal in the real, the invasion of the intelligible by the unintelligible. The very presence of the unintelligible makes the political approach—as well as the sociological or psychological—inadequate. To present man as merely social, the way Ionesco feels that Brecht presents him, is to truncate him: "What obsesses me personally, what interests me profoundly, what I am committed to is the problem of the human condition as a whole, in its social and non-social aspects. It is in its non-social aspect that man is profoundly alone. Faced with death, for example. Then society no longer counts" (*NCN* 140–41). This metaphysical approach, which characterizes the theater of the absurd in general, places it, in relation to the realistic theater, in a somewhat similar position to that occupied by Kafka in relation to the psychological novel. "For the last time psychology!" says Kafka;[18] "Avoid psychology," says Ionesco, but he adds: "or rather give it a metaphysical dimension" (*NCN* 25). A psychology with a metaphysical dimension is precisely the type of psychology—the only type of psychology—that Kafka's heroes may be said to possess. They are men abstracted into metaphysical questers, "deprived of our distractions," as Camus put it.[19] And so are many Ionesco characters.

Their metaphysical quest has the unintelligible for its object: persecuting law, inaccessible castle, growing corpse, proliferating furniture. They desperately try to make it accessible with the help of their human thinking. They try to confront it with mackintoshes and doctors, solicitors, psychoanalysts, and police.[20] But the "logical" analysis of what is happening is drowned by the rhinoceroses' noises, and the Logician himself finally turns into a rhinoceros.[21] The New Tenant is entombed in a dungeon of furniture, and Amédée is carried off forever by the corpse-turned-parachute. The unintelligible makes its point rather rudely.

Ionesco's world, like Kafka's, is therefore strictly dualistic. Man inhabits a cosy region of human logic, medicine, psychoanalysis, and jurisprudence. He organizes his world in patterns and histories. Behind it all, however, a nonhuman blank looms. In his moving *Fragments of a Journal* Ionesco speaks of history as "a torrent of wrong answers" to an unanswerable Why?[22] or of the universe as a "storehouse of objects" flung into the immensity of an incomprehensible space.[23] The duality of familiar parts and unknown whole is repeated there in many variations: known laws versus unknown reason for the laws; or words and explanations versus the deepest meaning that is lost in them; or a flood of images, words, characters, symbolic figures, signs—a chaotic jumble of messages—versus the fundamental problem: What is this world?[24] "To know what there is beneath it all. That's the most important thing."[25]

To say that the absurd, at least in Ionesco's version, excludes transcendence—and hence that it excludes Kafka[26]—is therefore absurd. The old transcendental certainties are gone, but they are badly missed, passionately longed for. Being cut off from our transcendental roots, from the knowledge of "what there is beneath it all," is a leitmotif in Ionesco. And it is associated in his mind with Kafka, as shown by the only complete piece he wrote about him, an interpretation of "The City Coat of Arms."[27] The builders of the Tower of Babel sinned—that is how Ionesco explains Kafka's meaning—not in wishing to build the tower but, on the contrary, in not really wishing it. They were bogged down by secondary, materialistic goals (the French *"buts"* with a small b), like housing for the staff, trade union problems, and so on, and lost sight of the principal *"But,"* the "vue d'essentiel." Man has been ever since lost in a labyrinth without an Ariadne's thread: "coupé de ses racines religieuses ou métaphysiques ou transcendantales, l'homme est perdu, toute sa démarche devient insensée, absurde, inutile, étouffante."[28] Elsewhere, Ionesco criticizes the nouveau roman for dehumanizing man by presenting him as no longer even suffering from the fact that he is cut off from his roots.[29]

IV   The duality of known and unknown, parts and whole, fussy foreground and blank background, dominates the structure of Ionesco's work no less than it does Kafka's or Beckett's. Here again, the fact that he is a playwright and thinks in terms of the stage determines the form that this duality bears in his plays. What appears in Kafka as a proliferation of explanations around the inexplicable, and in Beckett as a proliferation of utterances around the unutterable, here becomes a proliferation of objects around an empty space. This is the stage equivalent.

The proliferation of objects in Ionesco's plays has often been discussed. This is natural enough, for it is one of his most persistent motifs. He himself mentions some glaring cases in a short essay, "The Starting Point":

> Countless mushrooms sprout in the flat of Amédée and Madeleine; a dead body suffering from "geometrical progression" grows there too and turns the tenants out; in *Victims of Duty*, when coffee is to be served to three of the characters, there is a mounting pile of hundreds of cups; the furniture in *The New Tenant* first blocks up every staircase in the building, then clutters the stage, and finally entombs the character who came to take a room in the house; in *The Chairs* the stage is

filled with dozens of chairs for invisible guests; and in *Jacques* several noses appear on the face of a young girl.[30]

Mushrooms, dead body, coffee cups, furniture, chairs, noses—one could add eggs (*The Future Is in Eggs*) and rhinoceroses (*Rhinoceros*) —are then explained as the materialization of "the victory of the anti-spiritual forces, of everything we are struggling against."[31] They are produced by a "state of consciousness" in which "the universe is crushing me," "matter fills every corner, takes up all the space" (one cannot but think of *Nausea*); "the world becomes a stifling dungeon"; "I am invaded by heavy forces."[32] They stand, in other words, for the extrahuman material world, or rather for the material world as it appears to man in a certain state of mind. This latter, projective aspect is the one emphasized in another essay, "Hearts Are Not Worn on the Sleeve": "I have attempted . . . to exteriorise, by using objects, the anguish . . . of my characters, to make the set speak and the action on the stage more visual, to translate into concrete images terror, regret or remorse, and estrangement."[33] Whether the enemy is the material world itself or one's terror of it, its proliferation is an image of the uncontrollable momentum it gathers. The corpse in *Amédée* and the furniture in *The New Tenant* clutter and choke the stage and leave no room for man. In a sense Ionesco's interpretation of Kafka's "The City Coat of Arms" is another version of the same: the housing for the staff gathers its own momentum and leaves no room for spiritual aspiration.

But surely Ionesco's use of his proliferating objects is more complex than that. If proliferation were mere synonym for overpowering and crushing, it would hardly deserve the repeated attention he has given it.

Take furniture, his favorite proliferating object. It crowds *The New Tenant* and *Amédée* until their protagonists are completely walled in, and in *The Chairs* it is both title and protagonist. Would it be too farfetched to mention that in "The Metamorphosis," too, furniture plays a considerable part? I don't think it would, for Kafka's use of furniture in Ionesco's favorite Kafka story sheds much light on Ionesco's own practice.

In "The Metamorphosis" Samsa's familiar room and furniture act as realistic foils for the rather unfamiliar event that takes place there. We have seen that in *The New Tenant,* too, the furniture that will soon behave most irregularly is described as "completely realistic." In both cases, with all differences I have pointed out, the interpenetration of the commonplace and the fantastic is what the authors aim at. But there is another resemblance, more relevant to our present concern. Both in the Kafka story and in *Amédée* and *The New Tenant,* what begins as a comforting metonymy of human life ends, through wild proliferation, as its opposite: dead matter, decline, suffocation. If in the first part of "The Metamorphosis" Samsa is clinging to his furniture as to his humanity, resisting his sister's intention to give full scope to his animality by taking the furniture out, in the last part, parallel to his decline, his room gradually becomes a lumber room. Like the speaker in Shakespeare's sonnet, he is "consum'd with that which [he] was nourish'd by." The same holds for the Ionesco plays. In *Amédée* the scanty furniture of act 1 (during the main part of which the dead body is still safely hidden in the next room) proliferates in act 2 until Amédée and his wife are "barely visible, concealed by the lumber" (*A* 31). The dead man has taken up all the space by now. Carried out to the street, he is liable to leave "no room for the lorries to pass" (*A* 69). This, of course, is what the furniture actually does in *The New Tenant.* The two very small stools (*NT* 98), carefully positioned in the empty room and inspected with a satisfied look, even admired (*NT* 100), slowly but monstrously proliferate until the new tenant is entombed (*NT* 112). When we last see him only his hat shows from within the lumber enclosure. Then the two furniture movers put out the light. I can't help thinking of the two executioners in *The Trial.* The tenant himself, a perfect gentleman dressed in black clothes, wearing a bowler hat, and carrying a black attaché case, cannot but remind one of Joseph K.

The comparison with "The Metamorphosis" thus brings out certain aspects in Ionesco's use of furniture that are subtler, more paradoxical than meets the eye. Furniture *is* what Ionesco says it is—"everything we are struggling against," "a stifling dungeon"— but it first gave comfort and cosiness, and it might ironically give it to the very end. "It's good to feel at home," the tenant says when already walled in completely (*NT* 113). He obviously wants to be walled in, wants to block up the window with the sideboard and shut out the light (*NT* 108), wants the picture to be turned around and the radio not to work (*NT* 109, 111), wants them, that is, as protection from, not reminders of, the outside world. Objects multiply, therefore, not only as a materialization of the outer world, but also as a human defense against it.

Furniture, of course, is human in the simple sense that it is man-made. In the article quoted earlier Professor Doubrovsky claims that Ionesco's objects are "for the most part of human fabrication," and that their uncontrollable growth conveys "both the futility of man's attempt to give himself through boundless material production the fullness of being which he lacks, and the inevitable ultimate triumph of object over subject."[34] Although I cannot agree that Ionesco's objects are "for the most part" man-made (for example, dead body, mushrooms, noses, eggs, rhinoceroses), furniture most certainly is, and its proliferation may definitely be intentional, a human search for what will compensate for the void within. Perhaps a less literal reading than Doubrovsky's would go beyond "material production" to mental production, to the human production of fictions as compensation for the unknowable blank. The central text in this connection is *The Chairs*. The main inspiration—Kafka.

V   That Kafka lets human explanations, comments, exegeses, and legends proliferate around the "inexplicable mass of rock" needs no proof at this point. Nor is it necessary to refer again to Walter Benjamin's description of Kafka's work as *Aggadah* with no *Halakhah*, lacking the doctrine of which it should have served as commentary. What I should like to consider now is how this applies to *The Chairs*.

Furniture in general, but chairs in particular, are naturally metonymic, or rather synecdochic, for they immediately call for completion by the person who uses them. That is why an unused chair, like an archaic torso, is a constant reminder of absence. The growing corpse in *Amédée* may be a reminder of dead love, of a dead past; the accumulating furniture in *The New Tenant* may be a reminder of products made by man as defense against a terrifying world; both, at all events, are reminders of what *is* (or was). The chairs in *The Chairs* are a reminder of what is *not*.

Ionesco, of course, is perfectly aware of this paradox. Discussing the play, he speaks of "the presence of this absence," of "plenty of . . . moving objects . . . to create this emptiness," of "intangible presence," of a "tightly-packed crowd of non-existent beings,"[35] of "this nothing that is on the stage" (*NCN* 196, 197, 200). Absence being the point of the play, it is a metaphysical, not psychological, play. It is about the ontological void beyond the façade of being, not about the mental makeup of an old couple cherishing a delusion à la *Who's Afraid of Virginia Woolf?* This is how Ionesco put it in a conversation with Claude Bonnefoy:

> I understood [the meaning of *The Chairs*] a little sooner than the critics who said: "This play is the story of two failures. Their life, and life in general, is failure, and absurdity. These two old people—who've never managed to achieve anything, who imagine that they're receiving guests—they think they exist, they try to delude themselves, to persuade themselves that they actually have something to say. . . ." In other words, the critics and spectators simply described the play's subject-matter. But that wasn't really the point of the play. It was something quite different: it was the chairs themselves, and what the chairs meant—well, I've tried to understand it, but it's like trying to interpret one's own dreams. I've said to myself: That's it, it's absence, emptiness, nothingness. The chairs remain empty because there's no one there . . . there's nothing. The world doesn't really exist . . . the play itself consisted of empty chairs, and more chairs arriving, a whirlwind of them being brought on and taking over the whole stage as if a massive, all-invading void was settling in. . . . On this initial image, on this first obsession, I grafted the story of an old couple who are themselves on the verge of nothingness, and who

have had problems all their lives. But their story is intended merely to support the initial, fundamental image which gives the play its meaning . . . [their] ordinariness . . . sets off or accentuates all that's not ordinary, all that's unusual, strange or symbolic . . . there is this movement, this abstract whirlwind of chairs, while the two old people act as the pivot for a pure construction, for the moving architecture that a play really is; similarly in *Amédée* where there's the real corpse and the two characters who seem to exist.[36]

If the play is metaphysical, not psychological, and if its real protagonists are the chairs, not the old couple, then the fantastic is more real than the realistic, and emptiness is truer than gesture, sound, moving doors, and characters. But were it not for gesture, sound, moving doors, and characters, the "massive void" would not be there. The presence of real emptiness depends on that of the unreal characters—or, for that matter, of the unreal chairs.

This paradox is profoundly Kafkaesque. The four legends, we have seen, are evoked in Kafka's "Prometheus" only to be withdrawn and thereby lead to the inexplicable mass of rock that underlies them. The long commentary on the parable "Before the Law" is made by the priest only to point out to Joseph K. that one "must not pay too much attention" to it. Every single act made by all three K.s—Karl Rossmann, Joseph K., and K.—is made only to be unmade. The blank needs a lot of fuss to assert itself.

Ionesco's chairs are the equivalent of Kafka's legends. They are the *Aggadah* commenting on nothing. They are a reminder that all those invited, all the characters, all the property owners, all the intellectuals, the janitors, the bishops, the chemists, the tinsmiths, the violinists, the delegates, the presidents, the police, the merchants, the buildings, the pen holders, the chromosomes, the post office employees, the innkeepers, the artists, the bankers, the proletarians, the functionaries, the militaries, the revolutionaries, the reactionaries, the alienists, and their alienated, "all of them, all of them, all of them"[37] will never arrive. Forming regular rows as in a theater,[38] they are a reminder that the play (*The Chairs* itself?), the theme, the message will never[39] materialize, or, if it does, will cancel itself out by combining God's fullness with God's negation and with farewell.[40]

In a note to *Exit the King,* included in *Fragments of a Journal,* there is a section that enacts the regression from legend to absence, from the palace of fiction to the desert beyond it. In this it follows Kafka's "Prometheus." Unlike Borges's "A Problem," which also follows the same model,[41] there is no consolation here. Ionesco faces the desert with a humility typical, paradoxically, of this virtuoso writer:

> A guide is taking visitors or tourists round the Throne Rooms, or showing them a white funeral monument.
> *The Guide:* Ladies and gentlemen, boys and girls, ten minutes ago our great King Bérenger was living here . . . A hundred years ago, our great King Bérenger lived here . . . Ten thousand years ago, a great king called Bérenger lived here with his court . . . It is said that twenty thousand years ago men were already civilized and lived under a king whose name was said to be Bérenger . . . Ladies and gentlemen, according to legend there was once a palace here in which a king lived. Archaeologists have dug the site. But in fact nobody ever lived here. The place has always been a desert.[42]

7

A Sacred Latrine Called Qaphqa:
Borges's Kafkaism

I In his afterword to *The Book of Sand* (1975), Borges says of his story "The Congress" that: "Its opaque beginning tries to imitate that of a Kafka story; its end tries, doubtless in vain, to match the ecstasies of Chesterton and John Bunyan."[1]

These words, as so often with Borges, implicitly refer the reader to another text by the same author. The juxtaposition of Kafka, Chesterton, and Bunyan becomes clearer by reference to Borges's essay "On Chesterton," included in *Other Inquisitions* (1960). There, he describes Chesterton as a writer leaning toward the nightmarish, but subjecting his "demoniacal will" to religious faith. Two opposing parables represent the poles between which Chesterton is torn: Kafka's "Before the Law" and a passage from *Pilgrim's Progress* in which man fights the warriors guarding a castle, defeats them, and enters. "Chesterton," Borges concludes, "devoted his life to the writing of the second parable, but something within him always tended to write the first."[2]

Thus, if the end of "The Congress" tries in vain to match the ecstasies of Chesterton, Chesterton's own ecstasies are halfhearted, the forceful suppression of a basically Kafkaesque sensibility. But what is this type of sensibility? What is the Kafkaesque to Borges?

The opposition between the two parables implies a rather trite answer: the Kafkaesque is the failure of a quest plus, perhaps, the reason for this failure: reluctance to act, passivity, cowardice. For unlike Bunyan's "intrepid man," Kafka's sits down and waits, and presumably for this reason he never enters the door destined for him alone.

This sense of "Kafkaesque" hardly applies to "The Congress," though. "The Congress" is not really the story of a failed quest. Perhaps Borges means something less specific. He calls the beginning that tries to imitate Kafka "opaque"; and in the Chesterton essay he describes the parable "Before the Law" as "complicated" (*OI* 85). Perhaps the Kafkaesque, for Borges, is what is opaque and complicated. Thus, the beginning of "The Congress" would imitate Kafka simply by being opaque and complicated.

But this will not do. Borges's lifelong preoccupation with Kafka —he has translated, introduced, anthologized, commented on, and quoted from him—must have produced (or been produced by) a much more accurate concept of the Kafkaesque. Let me try, before returning to "The Congress" and to Kafka's possible influence on Borges's fiction, to outline this concept as it emerges from Borges's direct references to Kafka's work.

In an early essay he rejects all symbolic or allegorical reading of Kafka, calling his stories "disinterested dreams," "nightmares without any reason except their enchantment."[3] But enchantment, to Borges, is never divorced from ratiocination. What is notable about Kafka's dreams is not only their imagery but their peculiar logic. Thus, if in his *Book of Imaginary Beings* Borges includes Kafka's purely fantastic "Odradek" or "Crossbreed,"[4] in another anthology, *Extraordinary Tales*, he includes "The Silence of the Sirens," "The Truth about Sancho Panza," and four of the "Reflections on Sin, Pain, Hope, and the True Way," texts that can hardly be described as "disinterested dreams."[5]

The texts by Kafka that Borges selected for inclusion in *Extraordinary Tales* show what he found important or striking in Kafka the thinker rather than Kafka the dreamer. So does his important essay "Kafka and His Precursors" (1951; *OI* 106).[6] What are the main ideas he associates with the Kafkaesque, according to the anthology and the essay?

They can all be referred, it seems, to a central concern: the collapse of myth, ritual, and faith. The two longer texts selected for *Extraordinary Tales*, "The Silence of the Sirens" and "The Truth about Sancho Panza," as well as "Prometheus," which Borges translated, are all obvious reversals of myth. The first gives the Sirens the weapon of silence and turns Ulysses into either a simpleton or the ultimate fox.[7] The second turns Don Quixote into the imagined double of Sancho Panza.[8] The third reduces the Prometheus myth into a "meaningless affair." The original sense of myth is no longer acceptable. It is, in fact, lost. There are no kings around, as the fourth of the "Reflections" included in the anthology puts it; the king's couriers are posting through the world, shouting to each other their meaningless messages.

One element in the reversal of myth is that arrival and achievement become nonarrival and nonachievement. The parable "Before the Law" mentioned in the Chesterton essay is one example. It is "complicated," as Borges puts it, because arrival is potentially possible (the door "was destined for you alone"), and the fact that it has not occurred is therefore doubly cruel. The same holds for the unicorn in the ninth-century Chinese apologue mentioned as one of Kafka's precursors: everybody knows it is a "supernatural being of good omen," but one could be face-to-face with it and not recognize it (*L* 234–35).[9] The stories by Léon Bloy and Lord Dunsany, also mentioned as Kafka's precursors, are likewise emblems of nonarrival: the first tells of a city that is never left, the second of a city that is never reached (*L* 235–36).

The "logical" basis for nonarrival is provided by Zeno's paradox against movement: "The moving object and the arrow and Achilles," says Borges in "Kafka and His Precursors," "are the first Kafkian characters in literature." The form of *The Castle,* he says, is exactly that of this "illustrious problem," according to which "a moving object at A cannot reach point B because it must first cover half the distance between the two points, and before that, half of the half, and before that, half of the half of the half, and so on to infinity" (*L* 234).[10] Thus, *Regressus in infinitum,* a central structural principle in Borges's work, is located in Kafka. That "infinite postponement" is the central motif in Kafka had been Borges's view as early as in the prologue to his translation of selected stories by Kafka, published in 1938.[11]

Beyond nonarrival and failure, however, Borges finds in Kafka two further ideas that may be seen as solutions or comforts, though in a most complex sense. The one is implied in a strange parable by Kierkegaard, a parable Borges views as another precursor of Kafka:

Danish ministers had declared from their pulpits that participation in [the North Pole] expeditions was beneficial to the soul's eternal well-being. They admitted, however, that it was difficult, and perhaps impossible to reach the Pole and that not all men could undertake the adventure. Finally, they would announce that any trip—from Denmark to London, let us say, on the regularly scheduled steamer—was, properly considered, an expedition to the North Pole. (*L* 235)

Here, too, the quest must end in failure: the North Pole is probably unreachable. Miraculously, however, the unreachable becomes ubiquitous. Any trip is announced to be an expedition to the North Pole; any step, when "properly considered," leads to salvation. The Kafkaesque element here is elusive; Borges does not specify which work by Kafka he has in mind. Still, one feels he is right. The half-ironic transformation of nowhere into everywhere, negation into affirmation, is pure Kafka.

Another solution, perhaps related to the same, is offered by the first of Kafka's four "Reflections" included in *Extraordinary Tales*: "Leopards break into the temple and drink the sacrificial chalices dry; this occurs repeatedly, again and again: finally it can be reckoned upon beforehand and becomes a part of the ceremony" (*ET* 139).[12] The destruction of ritual here is integrated into ritual and thus overcome: a rich insight that may be applied, for instance, to the history of established religion and the way it has coped with heresy. Or, theologically, it may refer to the *via negativa*, to the way God must include his negation to be all-inclusive. The dialectics of negation-affirmation is once again the purport of this aphorism— and what may have made Borges select it for *Extraordinary Tales*.

II   To return to "The Congress," what makes it truly Kafkaesque in parts is neither some general "opaqueness" nor the specific resemblances to Kafka's *The Castle* that critics have detected.[13] It is rather its adoption of the last two motifs we found in Borges's Kafka image. These two paradoxical motifs—they can be called the paradox of the "commonplace secret" and the paradox of "negation as part of affirmation"—can be shown further to reverberate throughout Borges's work, notable for its repetitions and inter-references. The variations on the two paradoxes are one element of unity in Borges's highly unified oeuvre.

To take what I call the "commonplace secret" first, its relation to Kafka is amusingly hinted at in the "sacred latrine called Qaphqa," which in the story "The Lottery in Babylon" is supposed by general opinion to lead to the secret "Company" (*L* 58). The oxymoron of "sacred latrine" blatantly yokes together the highest and the lowest—not, I think, to cast dirt on the holy, but as part of the story's paradoxical cast. For it is a story that oscillates between the esoteric and the universal, making the omnipotent Company both secret and ubiquitous, and, furthermore, presenting this paradox as logically inevitable: that which is unknown can be anywhere, a secret law can be manifested in anything: "The drunkard who improvises an absurd order, the dreamer who awakens suddenly and strangles the woman who sleeps at his side, do they not execute, perhaps, a secret decision of the Company?" (*L* 60). Since the lottery adminis-tered by the Company is "an interpolation of chance in the order of the world" (*L* 58), it may show in anything—or in nothing. The way the "shadowy corporation" itself is consequently said both to be eternal and to have never existed, or to be both omnipotent and to have influence only in tiny things (*L* 60–61), is strongly reminiscent of the logic of Kafka's short text "The Problem of Our Laws." There, too, the speaker oscillates between belief in the laws and a skepticism that derives from their secrecy. Their existence is both postulated as indispensable and dismissed as an "intellectual game" (*CS* 437). They are both everywhere and nowhere.

This paradox, only suggested and variously implied in Kafka, becomes typically explicit and uniform in Borges. I say typically because Kafka's "irreducible and enigmatic situations," as James E. Irby has put it so well, "contrast strongly with Borges's compact but vastly significant theorems, his all-dissolving ratiocination."[14] Thus, the Company of "The Lottery in Babylon" reappears as the Sect in "The Sect of the Phoenix" (*L* 131), or as the Congress in "The Congress." All three—Company, Sect, and Congress—are interchangeable in their paradoxical combination of secrecy and triviality. The members of the Sect of the Phoenix call themselves "the People of the Secret," but they are "indistinguishable from the rest of the world," resemble "all the men in the world," and identify themselves "with all the nations of the earth" (*L* 131–32). Theirs is a secret cult, but it may be celebrated anywhere, any cellar or entrance hall will do (*L* 133). Likewise the Congress, a "Congress of the World" of which "all men are members" (*BS* 16–17), is also limited to a single member, the narrator himself (*BS* 16); and to see the true Congress is to be taken by the driver "anywhere [he] likes" (*BS* 32–33). Any trip—to go back to Borges's Kafkaesque Kierkegaard—is an expedition to the North Pole.

Although Borges is certainly right in regarding Kierkegaard's parable as Kafkaesque, it would be much harder to find three such variations on this theme in Kafka himself. It would be hard indeed to find even a single case as explicit and well defined as Borges's Company, Sect, or Congress. For Kafka paints "pictures, only pictures,"[15] he invents situations—"situaciones intolerables" Borges calls them[16]—which may be simplified into ideas but which remain irreducible fundamentally. Borges, on the other hand, seems to have ideas first and then find images to embody them.[17] When the idea he has is that "the Secret is anywhere," he can use either Company, Sect, or Congress to make it concrete.

Those situations in Kafka that seem to imply the same thing are, on the contrary, strikingly different from one another. It is only at a very high level of abstraction that their affinity shows. For the sake of symmetry let us take three such situations.

The first is from *The Trial*. Tired of his advocate, K. plans to write his own defense. His crime being unknown to him, his self-defense must cover all important events in his life (*T* 126). It may thus happen to hit on what is relevant. But the fact that it covers his entire life can also mean that guilt is inherent in life as such. The secret, which in this case is the secret of guilt, is both somewhere and anywhere.

In the similarly legal context of the short text "Advocates" (1922), the distant noise—often associated in Kafka with the unknown—comes simultaneously from everywhere and from just the spot where one happens to be standing: "What reminded me of a law court more than all the details was a droning noise which could be heard incessantly in the distance; one could not tell from which direction it came, it filled every room to such an extent that one had to assume it came from everywhere, or, what seemed more likely, that just the place where one happened to be standing was the very place where the droning originated" (*CS* 449).

Finally, in the climactic chapter 18 of *The Castle,* to which we have referred more than once, K. is finally given the secret message, which turns out to be a mere pointing to what is happening: there it is. The way to salvation is both infinitely unknown and inherent in any immediately given moment.

The parallelism with the Kierkegaard parable is manifest. So is the parallelism with Borges. Except that what in Kafka is part of the *condition humaine* and of experience becomes, in Borges, a discursive idea clad in images.

III   The discursiveness of Borges shows in the neatness with which the "commonplace secret" paradox can be integrated into the larger body of his thought. That which in Kafka is a cry of anguish—What is guilt? Where is salvation?—here becomes an elegant reconciliation between two opposed quests.

The two quests can be called *progressus ad infinitum* and *regressus ad infinitum,* or the *via affirmativa* and the *via negativa.* Both aim at the undecipherable secret of being, but the first does so by accumulation, the second by elimination.

In the afterword to *The Book of Sand* the two are explicitly contrasted: "Two opposite and inconceivable concepts are the subjects of the last two stories. 'The Disk' is about the Euclidean circle, which has only one side; 'The Book of Sand,' a volume of incalculable pages" (*BS* 93–94). The disk, the only thing in the world with only one side, is lost; the narrator is still searching for it (*BS* 86). The Book of Sand—called so "because neither the book nor the sand has any beginning or end" (*BS* 89)—is likewise lost, on one of the musty shelves in the basement of the Argentine National

Library (*BS* 91). The two opposite concepts—the unique and the all-embracing, the infinitesimal and the infinite—are equally out of reach.

Many of Borges's stories arrange themselves, directly or indirectly, under one of these two rubrics. "Funes the Memorious" (*L* 87), for instance, whose memory is "like a garbage heap," preserving every concrete item, is a grotesque emblem of accumulation ad infinitum. In "The Zahir" (*L* 189) or the "Parable of the Palace,"[18] on the other hand, the movement is inward rather than outward: toward the single coin, the single word, that which is absolutely unique.

Behind the single coin, however, one may find God (*L* 197), and the single word contains all the enormous palace in its most minute details (*PA* 88). In "The Aleph" millions of acts occupy the same point and are simultaneous in it (*PA* 150). Elimination, thus, is only seemingly opposed to accumulation. In the final analysis it likewise aims at totality.

What I call the paradox of the commonplace secret is the combination of the singular and the universal, of elimination and accumulation. Since one cannot tell where the secret resides, it may reside anywhere. All things become charged with secrecy, but secrecy itself becomes charged with banality and may prove trivial at any minute. The latrine called Qaphqa may be sacred, but sacredness may be no more than a latrine.

Texts such as "The God's Script" (*L* 203) or "Paradiso, XXXI, 108" (*L* 274) enact this paradox: they move from the lost unique to the commonplace unique. In "The God's Script" the secret magical sentence written by God on the first day of creation, a sentence with the power to ward off ruin, may reside in any shape anywhere on the earth, may be written on the narrator's own face—"perhaps I myself was the end of my search." In "Paradiso, XXXI, 108" the lost face of Jesus may reappear in "a Jew's profile in the subway," in "every mirror," in "all of us." One notes that in both texts the knowledge of the secret—like the passage to the law in "Before the Law" or the appearance of the redemptive unicorn in the Chinese apologue—is potentially possible, and one possibility is that the search will end in oneself. The claustrophobic implications of this last possibility, being locked in a cabinet of mirrors, unable to reach the world beyond one's projections, are central to Kafka[19] and not unknown to Borges.[20]

In "The Congress" the paradox of the commonplace secret becomes very central indeed. It is there already in the epigraph from Diderot that tells of a great castle on whose façade are carved the words "Je n'appartiens à personne et j'appartiens à tout le monde" (*BS* 15). The Congress also belongs to no one and to all, for all men are its members and yet the narrator is its "last member" (*BS* 16). This contradiction is immediately modified (the very technique of constant self-cancellation is Kafkaesque) when the narrator says that he is a member "in a very different way" from all the others, as he *knows* he is a member. Nevertheless, the paradox persists and is repeated in various guises: anyone's history is the history of the Congress of the World (*BS* 28); or the idea of the Congress was conceived by Glencoe but it also "began with the first moment of the world" (*BS* 20, 32); or the Congress is meant to meet at Glencoe's ranch in Uruguay but "there's no place on earth where it does not exist" (*BS* 21, 32). Singularity and ubiquity, both in time and space, are constantly yoked together. The Congress is both the most exclusive of clubs and the world itself.

The logical difficulty of being both is reflected in a "problem of a philosophical nature": "Planning an assembly to represent all men was like fixing the exact number of Platonic types" (*BS* 21). Representation involves the reduction of the world's plenitude to categories, to "Platonic types," and this requires a principle of classification. But what is it? What are the human types to be represented in the Congress? Should Glencoe, for instance, "represent not only cattlemen but also Uruguayans, and also humanity's great forerunners, and also men with red beards, and also those who are seated in armchairs" (ibid.)?

The same question applies to the "analytical language" that was devised in the seventeenth century by John Wilkins, a short study of which the narrator says he has published (*BS* 16). Being a language "in which the definition of each word is to be found in the letters that spell it out," that is, a nonarbitrary language in which signifiers are naturally related to signifieds, it might be "a language worthy of the Congress of the World" (*BS* 28). To understand Wilkins's relevance to "The Congress" one must turn once again to another Borges text. For not only Ferri, the narrator of "The Congress," but Borges himself has published a short study of Wilkins—"The Analytical Language of John Wilkins," included in *Other Inquisitions*. To invent his "expressive" (what linguists would call "naturally motivated") language, Wilkins, says Borges, had to divide the world into categories, subdivisible into differences, subdivisible into species. But "obviously there is no classification of the universe that is not arbitrary and conjectural. The reason is very simple: we do not know what the universe is. . . . But the impossibility of penetrating the divine scheme of the universe cannot dissuade us from outlining human schemes, even though we are aware that they are provisional" (*OI* 104).

This universal language—like the universal Congress—involves the question of representation, and hence of classification, and hence of the very structure of the universe, its "divine scheme." The divine scheme being unknowable, classification and representation are impossible except provisionally. To be more than provisional, language would have to do without classification into categories; it would have to have a separate sign for every individual item. Such would be the language acceptable to Funes the Memorious: "Not only was it difficult for him to comprehend that the generic symbol *dog* embraces so many unlike individuals of diverse size and form; it bothered him that the dog at three fourteen (seen from the side) should have the same name as the dog at three fifteen (seen from the front)" (*L* 93–94). So incapable is Funes of "ideas of a general, Platonic sort," that he calls numbers by proper names such as "sulphur," "the gas," or "Napoleon" (*L* 93).

By analogy, the Congress—the language or text of the world, if you will—can represent the world only by including it all, by being it. We are back to the paradox of the commonplace secret. The secret is commonplace, we said, because it is unknowable and therefore potentially anywhere; the secret is commonplace, we can add now, because the divine scheme of the universe is unknowable, and therefore classification and representation are impossible, and therefore an account of things must include them all. It is like the map of the empire that turns out to be the size of the empire itself.[21]

In the last pages of "The Congress" this cerebral paradox becomes experience. Glencoe invites his colleagues to go out together to see the Congress and orders the driver to take them *anywhere he likes* (*BS* 32–33). The Congress is anywhere—it is in "the reddish wall of the Recoleta cemetery, the yellow wall of a jail, a couple of men dancing together at a right-angled street corner, a church courtyard with black-and-white tiles and a grilled iron fence, a railway gate crossing, my house, a marketplace, the damp unfathomable night": the Congress is all these, but "none of these fleeting things, which may have been others, now matter. What really matters is having felt that our plan, which more than once we made a joke of, really and secretly existed and was the world and ourselves" (*BS* 33).

The reality of the secret plan, of the world, of the self, is both anchored in certain fleeting things and independent of them: they may have been others.[22] One is reminded of Kierkegaard: "any trip was, properly considered, an expedition to the North Pole," and of Kafka: "it filled every room to such an extent that one had to assume it came from everywhere, or, what seemed more likely, that just the place where one happened to be standing was the very place where the droning originated."

IV   The other Kafkaesque paradox that seems important to Borges is what I called, rather awkwardly, "negation as part of affirmation." The leopards' intrusion on the ceremony, in Kafka's aphorism included in Borges's anthology, becomes part of the ceremony. The leopards may be said to affirm the ceremony in destroying it; but they may also be said to destroy the ceremony in affirming it. By extension, God, to be all-inclusive, must include his negation; to be affirmed he must be negated. The dialectics of affirmation-negation implied in this aphorism reminds one of Bürgel's final words in chapter 18 of *The Castle*, the words that crown his tortuous oscillation between the possibility and impossibility of getting to the Castle: "Only there are, of course, opportunities that are, in a manner of speaking, too great to be made use of, there are things that are wrecked on nothing but themselves" (*C* 255).[23] Endless opportunity begets its own negation.

This paradox, even more than the previous one, becomes far more explicit and systematic in Borges than it is in Kafka. What is only suggested in the precursor is rewritten as both theme and structural principle in many stories by his descendant.

As theme, the idea that totality must include negation is applied, for instance, to another symbol of the universe, the "Library of Babel." So "total" is the library that one can find on its shelves not only its own "faithful catalogue," but also "thousands and thousands of false catalogues, the demonstration of the fallacy of those catalogues, the demonstration of the fallacy of the true catalogue" (*L* 81) and so on ad infinitum, I suppose. Similarly, the totality of the Congress means that even though Ferri, the narrator, has sworn never to reveal its history, the fact that he *is* writing its history and committing perjury "is also part of the Congress" (*BS* 16). It also explains why the burning of the Congress's books is the Congress (*BS* 32). This last point is further clarified by reference to another Borges text: in "The Wall and the Books" (*PA* 89) it turns out that the same emperor who ordered the burning of books also built the Great Wall of China, and that both acts were designed to hold back death: in space (the wall stopping the enemy) and in time (the burning of books as destroying history, the past, time). Thus, to affirm the Congress's totality, its library must be negated, and the negation of the library is the affirmation of life, et cetera, et cetera.

In "From Someone to No One" (*PA* 118) negation is not only included in totality but identical with it. A historical survey of the "magnification" of God—and of Shakespeare—is said to show that both creators were first flooded with attributes, then deprived of them all when their worshippers came to the conclusion that "not to be . . . is to be everything" (*PA* 120). This "magnification to the point of nothingness" (*PA* 119) becomes literal in another text, "Everything and Nothing" (*L* 284): there is, it turns out, "no one" in Shakespeare, and neither is God "anyone." Both are "many and no one."

While in the first of these two texts God and Shakespeare are treated as two parallel cases, in the second there is a progressive—or rather regressive—structure: from the author Shakespeare as "no one" to his own author God as "no one." A similar regressive structure can be found in "The Circular Ruins" (*L* 72): from the child as "a mere image" to his father as "a mere appearance"; or in "The Sham" (*DT* 31): from the pretender who is not Perón to Perón who is not Perón. There is only one step to the final negation of the text itself, as in "From Someone to No One": "Schopenhauer has written that history is an interminable and perplexed dream on the part of generations of humans; in the dream there are recurring forms; perhaps there are nothing but forms; *one of them is the process described on this page*" (*PA* 121; my italics). There is much in common between this final negation of the text itself and Kafka's "An Imperial Message" from "The Great Wall of China," translated by Borges and briefly paraphrased in the prologue to his collection of Kafka translations. There, too, the messenger's journey, already negated in the text itself, is retroactively reduced, in the last sentence, to a dream: "But you sit at your window when evening falls and dream it to yourself" (*CS* 244).

But the most interesting formal expression in Borges of the dialectics of affirmation-negation is the type of text that consists of several versions or interpretations of a single discourse.[24] There again, Kafka's influence is manifest.

The connection between our paradox and this particular text structure can be best illustrated by "Forms of a Legend" (*PA* 122). The progressive negation of the original fable—its characters, then the world, then Buddha himself—takes place as its various versions unfold. Paradoxically, the more they affirm, the more they negate: "the vast forms . . . are only vast and monstrous bubbles, emphasizing Nothingness" (*PA* 127). Finally, the very account of the various versions is negated in its turn: "I should not be surprised if my story of the legend were legendary" (ibid.).

The multiversion story is a favorite with Borges. Such are "Three Versions of Judas" (*L* 125), "A Problem" (*L* 280), and "Parable of the Palace" (*PA* 87), to mention just a few. They are all related to the dialectics of negation-affirmation in that they both accumulate versions and interpretations and let them cancel each other out. That they are modeled on Kafka can be seen from a comparison between "A Problem" and Kafka's "Prometheus" (*CS* 432).[25] The structure of the two pieces is similar. Both take a classical figure—Prometheus, Don Quixote—and offer four alternative versions of his story (Prometheus), or of an episode from his story (Quixote). Both story and episode involve crime: betraying the secret of the gods to men in the case of Prometheus, killing a man in the case of Quixote. Their concern, thus, is presumably moral. By the time we get to the fourth and last version, however, moral concern dissolves into nothingness. Prometheus's treachery is "forgotten by the gods, the eagles, forgotten by himself." Finally, everyone grows weary of the "meaningless affair," the gods, the eagles, the wound. Don Quixote, in his turn, knows in the end that "the dead man is illusory, the same as the bloody sword weighing in his hand and himself and all his past life and the vast gods and the universe."

The resemblance is striking. The legend that "tried to explain the inexplicable," to quote "Prometheus," must "end in the inexplicable." In another piece on Quixote, "Parable of Cervantes and the *Quixote*" (*L* 278), Borges may be said to paraphrase these very words: "For in the beginning of literature is the myth, and in the end as well."

V   The multiple versions of myth in the two texts as well as their regression to nothingness or to the inexplicable, bring us back to the collapse of faith in which, I have argued, Borges's concept of Kafka centers. More accurately, they imply a situation in which the one truth, the original doctrine, is lost, and the ensuing perplexity leads to an infinite proliferation of exegeses. Kafka's above-mentioned "Reflection" about the king's couriers, included in Borges's *Extraordinary Tales*, offers a memorable image of this situation, of the divorce between parable and meaning. It often becomes explicit in Borges. I have quoted from "The Analytical Language of John

Wilkins," where "human schemes" are said to be constantly outlined, but only provisionally, for we can never penetrate the divine
scheme itself. In "The Mirror of Enigmas" Léon Bloy is quoted:
"History is an immense liturgical text where the iotas and the dots
are worth no less than the entire verses or chapters, but the importance of one and the other is indeterminable and profoundly hidden" (*L* 246). And in the short text "Pedro Salvadores," Pedro's
fate is said to be "a symbol of something we are about to understand but never quite do."[26] In all these texts symbols have lost
their power to refer to meanings.

Most explicit in this respect is "The Sect of the Phoenix." The
Sect's "secret" is the rite they perform, but the vision behind it—
the original legend or cosmogonic myth or divine verdict—is forgotten and survives in multiple versions that hide the truth: "Once,
in addition to the Secret, there was a legend (and perhaps a cosmogonic myth), but the shallow men of the Phoenix have forgotten
it and now only retain the obscure tradition of a punishment. Of a
punishment, of a pact or of a privilege, for the versions differ and
scarcely allow us to glimpse the verdict of a God who granted eternity to a lineage if its members, generation after generation, would
perform a rite" (*L* 132). This could serve as a perfect motto to Kafka
à la Benjamin. Borges has definitely learned his Kafka. And yet, it is
astonishing how different, in the final analysis, the two writers are.

Many of the differences have emerged during this discussion.
Kafka's "situaciones intolerables," totally irreducible, totally inseparable from narrative and image, too rich to be exhausted in ideas, let
alone in the homogeneity of a system, are rewritten in Borges as their
discursive parallels, largely separable from their multiple allegorical
guises, reducible to concepts, integrable in an overall scheme.
Borges, we have seen, speaks of the unknowability of the divine
scheme of the universe, but this unknowability, he says, "cannot
dissuade us from outlining human schemes." One could say, indeed,
that he is irreparably in love with human schemes, that he is much
too fascinated by them to be really worried by the loss of some
original cosmogonic myth, or to be truly harassed by the tragic
uncertainty of a Kafka. This is also his appeal: that of a brilliant
mind, ever surprising, ever sparkling, ever providing new comforts

for our lot, however sad. Not for him the final renouncement of human reason with which "The Metamorphosis" or *The Trial* ends.

That is also why the two multiversion stories we compared, "Prometheus" and "A Problem," are so different in spite of their striking similarities. Both regress to nothingness, but their nothingnesses are basically different.

> *Kafka:* According to the fourth [legend] everyone grew weary of the meaningless affair. The gods grew weary, the eagles grew weary, the wound closed wearily.
> There remained the inexplicable mass of rock. The legend tried to explain the inexplicable. As it came out of a substratum of truth it had in turn to end in the inexplicable. (*CS* 432)

> *Borges:* There is another conjecture, which is alien to the Spanish orb and even to the orb of the Western world and requires a more ancient, more complex and more weary atmosphere. Don Quixote—who is no longer Don Quixote but a king of the cylces of Hindustan—senses, standing before the dead body of his enemy, that killing and engendering are divine or magical acts which notably transcend the human condition. He knows that the dead man is illusory, the same as the bloody sword weighing in his hand and himself and all his past life and the vast gods and the universe. (*BS* 280–81)

What remains in Kafka, prior and posterior to all human schemes, is the inexplicable. What remains in Borges is another scheme, Eastern rather than Western, but still human, still a Weltanschauung. Illusionism, the influence of the Hindu scriptures, of Schopenhauer, explain much in Borges, particularly the dream that gradually envelops the hierarchy of being, step after step. Borges enjoys the comforts not only of a fascinating mind, but also of mystical experience. His Nothingness is capitalized, it is a rare gift, the ultimate achievement. Kafka's is a mass of rock, bare and comfortless.

8

History and the Law: S. Y. Agnon and Kafka

I   When a collection of five short stories by S. Y. Agnon entitled "The Book of Deeds" was first published in the literary supplement of the Hebrew daily *Davar* in Tel-Aviv on April 20, 1932, many brows were raised. To readers of Agnon—who would later be securely established as the dean of Hebrew novelists and awarded the 1966 Nobel Prize—"The Book of Deeds" seemed an aberration. In diametrical opposition to the sort of well composed, nostalgic, pious, though not necessarily idyllic tale they were used to, or thought they were used to, from Agnon, the dreamlike disorientation that marked these new stories seemed puzzling and pointless.[1] If an early story such as "Agunot" (1908) could be praised for its beautiful simplicity,[2] the "Book of Deeds" stories were far from simple. They were enigmatic and surrealistic.

In one of them, "To the Doctor,"[3] peas turned into lentils and a bridge quaked under the narrator's feet. In another, "The Document" (*TOS* 68–71), the narrator, pushed out of an office, found himself standing on a large porch floating on a vast sea. In still another, "Friendship" (*TOS* 72–78), the narrator was suddenly tongue-tied and could not get the name of his street out of his mouth. More stories, and more fantastic happenings, were added to "The Book of Deeds" in the following years. The final version, twenty stories in all, was included in the tenth volume (1950) of the first edition of Agnon's collected works.[4]

By then, if not much earlier, Agnon's image had been transformed. He could no longer be regarded as the sentimental extoller of the Jewish *shtetl* of Eastern Europe and its pieties. The gradual unfolding of the inner crisis of Judaism, and its horrifying enactment in World War II, brought into sharp focus the tension at the center of Agnon's work, a tension "between past and present, faith and atheism, art and life, innocence and irony."[5] "The Book of Deeds" now fell into place as a central work in Agnon's oeuvre. The most insistent exponent of the changed concept of Agnon, the Israeli critic Baruch Kurzweil, argued that it was precisely the surrealistic disorientation of "The Book of Deeds" that gave the most direct expression to modern perplexity, to the split between the holy and the demonic. It was this supposedly untypical work that provided to Kurzweil "the true psychological key for the understanding of Agnon's stories as a whole."[6]

Kurzweil concluded his essay with the suggestion that the "Book of Deeds" stories should be compared with Kafka. He was not the first, let alone the last, to notice an affinity between the two writers. Walter Benjamin, reading *The Trial* in the twenties, had suggested the possibility of a "Vergleich mit Agnon."[7] In a letter to Gershom Scholem dated January 18, 1934, he repeated the suggestion, choosing for special reference "The Big Synagogue" by Agnon, a story Scholem had translated into German.[8] It is a story about schoolchildren unearthing an old synagogue whose gate, unlike Kafka's gate to the law, opens to admit them. Inside, all the objects are intact: candlesticks, basin, ark; only the "eternal lamp" is about to go out. Among other things, it must have been the combination of physical presence and spiritual absence, or near absence, that suggested to Benjamin the affinity with Kafka—a combination that a few months later was to enter his great Kafka essay in the form of a dichotomy between existing *Aggadah* and nonexisting *Halakhah*.

The "Book of Deeds" stories, which Benjamin could not have known, were a new and much more obvious occasion for a comparison with Kafka. More obvious because of the new fantastic element that had entered Agnon's world, as well as the seeming disintegration of all coherent meaning. This is how Nahum Glatzer puts it in his postscript to a collection of Agnon's stories in English translation:

These surrealistic, introspective, dreamlike tales are told with a clarity and precision that remind some readers of Kafka's style. So, too, does the content: Man is lonely, homeless, in exile; meaning disintegrates, lines of communication break down; there is no exit. Deep faith is a matter of the past; the present forms of religion are full of ambivalence, paradox, even of decay. Time itself disintegrates. (*TOS* 277–78)

Homelessness, loneliness, meaninglessness, ambivalence, decay, all told with dreamlike lucidity: Glatzer's words sum up what is strikingly Kafkaesque about these stories. More particularly, one could add a narrative pattern that Agnon seems to share with Kafka. It is a pattern of a journey that leads to a cul-de-sac and consists of the following parts: departure from home, losing the way, a series of pointless encounters, missing all means of transportation, no return home. This pattern recurs in "The Book of Deeds" and is roughly analogous to the structure of *The Castle* or "The Country Doctor." It is the structure of what may be called a truncated myth, where a departure from routine existence and a passage to what is beyond it end not in an enriched return to the world, as in classical myth, but in being stranded in a no-man's-land between home and beyond. Thus, in Agnon's "To the Doctor" (*TOS* 65–67), the narrator leaves home to get a doctor for his sick father and little sister, is delayed by a Mr. Andermann ("other man," perhaps "other side," Sitra Akhra, one of the devil's names) and, crossing a bridge opposite the doctor's house, is about to drown in the river when the story abruptly ends. Or, in "A Whole Loaf" (*TOS* 79–95), the narrator leaves home to get some food, is delayed by a Dr. Ne'eman ("faithful", i.e., Moses, according to Kurzweil)[9] and a Mr. Gressler (Mephistopheles, says Kurzweil),[10] spends the night in a restaurant where he never gets the "whole loaf" he has ordered, and finds himself in the street when the story ends.

The infinite frustration thus inherent in what can usually be taken for granted—calling a doctor, getting food—is as central to Agnon as it is to Kafka. And the protagonist who suffers all this is likewise "a wholly passive figure, at the mercy of demonic or at least enigmatic forces that mock him or threaten to destroy him."[11]

Beyond such general similarities, however, one could point to certain details in Agnon's stories that seem directly borrowed from Kafka. Such is the opening of "To Father's House" (*TOS* 60–64) where two painters, like the two wardens at the beginning of *The Trial,* invade the narrator's home, sent, apparently, by some supernatural power to set in motion the narrator's quest. The end of the quest in "A Whole Loaf," on the other hand, where the protagonist, yearning for the "whole loaf," falls asleep on the floor of the restaurant and is awakened by the cleaners with their brooms in their hands, repeats a twofold motif from both "The Metamorphosis" and "The Hunger Artist": the yearning for unknown food ("the unknown nourishment" in the former story [*CS* 131], "the food I liked" in the latter [*CS* 277]) plus the protagonist's starved body found, poked at with broom or stick, and swept away (*CS* 136, 276). In "Edo and Enam," to bring a final example from a story not included in "The Book of Deeds," Kafka's attitude to the inexplicable mysteries of existence is applied to an act that seems borrowed from Kafka's own life. The scholar Dr. Ginath burns his papers before he dies and forbids his publishers to reprint his published work. As in the case of Kafka, his orders are ignored and his books are printed in increasing numbers. But why did Ginath burn his papers? It was psychological depression, some people say. The narrator, however, has his doubts:

> No explanations can affect the issue, no accounts of causes alter it. These are no more than the opinions people put forward in order to exercise their ingenuity in words without meaning on cases that cannot be solved, on happenings for which there is no solace. Even if we say that events are ordained from the beginning, we have not come to the end of the chain, and the matter is certainly not settled; nor does any knowledge of causes remove our disquiet.[12]

The impassable gap between our opinions and the inexplicable mystery of life seems borrowed from the priest's words to Joseph K. about the unalterable Scriptures and the comments as mere expressions of despair. The two authors have the same absurdist tension in mind: between the unalterable, comfortless "text" of being and the human need to explain it away in rational terms.[13] In what follows, however, I shall try to show that the resemblance between the two, though striking enough, is no more than skin deep.

II   One of the "Book of Deeds" stories, "Hefker" ("Abandon," 1945),[14] is uniquely rich with Kafkaesque echoes. Since it is particularly pertinent to my argument, and since it does not exist in English translation, I include an English version of it in the Appendix.

The Kafkan pattern I have mentioned as adopted by Agnon is evident in this story, too. Having left home, the narrator cannot return. He seems to have missed the last bus, is lost in a dark alley, is then led by a mysterious stranger to a strange room, and is waiting there for his verdict when the story ends. The atmosphere is dreamlike in parts, with logical coherence and causal links often gone. More specifically, three Kafkaesque elements stand out:

1. The theme of judgment. "The Hebrew writer, like the German [Kafka], is repeatedly concerned with the theme of judgment," writes Robert Alter. "His characters often find themselves peremptorily summoned before some sort of tribunal; their crucial experiences are set characteristically on the eve of the Jewish New Year or on the Day of Atonement, when Jews place themselves under the scrutiny of divine judgment."[15] "Abandon," for one, is not set on the eve of New Year or the Day of Atonement, but its narrator is likewise summoned before a tribunal. Or this is how he interprets the stranger's acts and words—the heavy hand that grasps his scarf, the "come along" that he utters—as well as those of the grotesque man reclining in bed. As in Kafka, and in our dreams, the boundaries between objective reality and subjective projection fall. The narrator's gradual acceptance of guilt may well be an autonomous psychic process that projects itself on outer reality.

2. The presumable "judge," reclining on a bed full of pillows and quilts, and confused as if just awakened from sleep, seems modeled on the secretary Bürgel of *The Castle* as well as on Georg Bendemann's father-judge in "The Judgement." His appearance, like Bürgel's, is preceded by a burning lamp (*C* 241), perhaps a parody

of the light of revelation. Bürgel, Bendemann's father, and Agnon's "judge" are all marked by ambivalence: of childishness and superior intellect in the first (*C* 241), of infantile helplessness and overbearing authority in Bendemann Senior (*CS* 81–84), of youth and age, faith (cantor's hat), and dictatorship (secret police) in Agnon's "judge." Above all, they all present a travesty of authority in the very fact that they receive the "defendant" in bed.

3. The obscene words sung to the prayer's melody by the old man and his companions in the last paragraph of "Abandon" are reminiscent of the startling combination of obscenity and the law in *The Trial*. The books Joseph K. finds on the Examining Magistrate's table are dirty, both literally and metaphorically. One has indecent pictures, another is a novel entitled "How Grete Was Plagued by Her Husband Hans" (*T* 60–61). Kafka's juxtaposition of the highest and the lowest could have inspired Agnon, though Jewish sources, as in the case of Kafka himself,[16] may also have been at work here.

III   "Abandon," in its general conception, structure, style, and some central motifs is thus strikingly Kafkaesque. But why did Agnon himself deny that Kafka was important to him? He did so quite vehemently in a letter to the Israeli critic Dov Sadan in 1962:

> I have never denied my debt to my masters nor have I kept secret my teachers, but "The Book of Deeds" was dictated to me by my innermost soul. It was my soul that told me these stories. Those who associate me with Kafka are quite mistaken. Before I published "The Book of Deeds" I had read no Kafka story except "The Metamorphosis," and to this very day I have not read any books by Kafka save *The Trial*—that was during an illness ten years ago. Many a time my wife has wanted to read a Kafka story to me, but without success, for after a page or two my mind wanders. Kafka is not close to my heart, and I cannot become absorbed in a writer who is not close to my heart, be he as great as the ten old men who wrote

the Book of Psalms. I know Kafka is a great poet, but he is a stranger to my heart.[17]

Writers are often reluctant to admit the influence of others. But there is no reason to assume that Agnon did not mean it when he said that Kafka was not close to his heart. After all, he did admit that Knut Hamsun's *Mysteries,* for example, had deeply impressed him.[18] The considerable links between "The Book of Deeds" and Kafka, though undeniable, are not necessarily an indication of real affinity between the two writers.

Going back to "Abandon," one notices that although there are supernatural elements in the story, they do not enter it until quite late. The first pages are strictly realistic, and it is only the heavy hand grasping the narrator's scarf that introduces the uncanny. Even that can still be motivated realistically. The supernatural proper appears only with the tomblike room that pops out of nowhere and the grotesque figure in bed.

With Kafka, it is often the other way around. He opens his stories with a supernatural event, but the rest of the story treats its results in perfectly realistic terms. Thus, both Samsa's metamorphosis and K.'s arrest take place in the first sentence (or even earlier) of their respective stories, while the rest of the story describes their repeated attempts to cope with a fantastically changed world.

But does the difference in order—first surreal then real in Kafka, first real then surreal in Agnon—matter? Isn't the very combination of the two, and the integration of the surreal into the real, what matters? It does, but the difference in order is significant in that it implies a difference in the status of the surreal. In Kafka it explodes out of nowhere and is therefore literal and irreducible. It is given as a hard, unyielding fact within Kafka's fictive universe, and its resistance to the terms of normal reality constitutes the plot of these stories. In Agnon the surreal gradually grows out of the mental state of his protagonists, presented realistically in the first part of the story. Even if it transcends their minds and becomes part of outer reality, it never loses its figurative status as a metaphor for the mind. Thus, in "Abandon" the tomblike room and the grotesque judge are products of the narrator's sense of guilt. As such, they are reducible to his mental state. They have come out of it and can be referred back to it; they form a continuum with reality. The surrealistic element in Agnon may therefore be said to be tentative: it exists only as long as its metaphorical meaning has not been deciphered.

One could use Todorov's terms again and say that, while Kafka sticks to the *merveilleux* (though in his own peculiar version, where it is incorporated into the banal), to Agnon the *merveilleux* is tentative and is soon replaced by *l'étrange*. In other words, Kafka's world, however realistic, allows for the intrusion of the irreducibly supernatural, whereas in Agnon the supernatural is soon explained realistically, leaving the laws of the universe unchanged.

But what is the mental state that produces the supernatural in "Abandon"? This is made amply clear in the first few paragraphs. It is a state of "hefker," abandon—freedom from constraint, particularly from religion[19] and one's responsibility to the community. Mr. Heilprin, who dominates the opening situation, is descended from a distinguished family of great scholars but has not learnt the Torah himself, and can only talk about his ancestors' beautiful homes and prosperous businesses. His friendship with the narrator reflects upon the latter and makes him a party to the spiritual decline that Heilprin embodies. The unsociable element in this decline, an alienation from the people and a giving up to egocentric impulses, is then symbolized in the narrator's choice of a quiet side street "not made for crowds," as well as in his inner refusal to help the man who is following him and who may be asking for help. Thus, neglect of the Torah, alienation from the people, egocentric seclusion (wrapping the scarf around his neck may symbolize this), and the passivity that he later enjoys when the "judge"'s stare rivets him to his place are the vices that account for the unconscious self-incrimination that will produce the fantasy of the trial in the last part of the story.

Thus, the surreal element in "Abandon"—and in "The Book of Deeds" as a whole—is the product of a well-defined guilt, well defined, that is, within the specific problematics of the Jewish people and their spiritual condition. Samsa's metamorphosis and Joseph K.'s arrest, on the other hand, resist all attempts to be interpreted as the proportionate punishment for a defined crime. Many such attempts have been made, of course. Samsa has been accused of being despotic, and Joseph K. of living a gray, unimaginative life. The disproportion, however, between such crimes and such punishments shows how pointless all such explanations are. Not only the nature of Samsa's or Joseph K.'s guilt, but its very existence remains doubtful. Is it their own guilt? Is it the world's? If the "man from the country" never arrives at the law, is it because he is a coward or because the doorkeepers *are* much too powerful? Agnon's answer would be unambiguous: the man from the country is passive, unsociable, and forgetful of the Torah. He is definitely guilty.

Not so his ancestors. The first paragraph of "Abandon" centers, though indirectly, on the decline from the illustrious early families who "sustained us during our long exile" to Mr. Heilprin, who has "studied secular sciences rather than the Torah." A historical process has led to the present situation. The crises in which the protagonists of "The Book of Deeds" find themselves are the result of great historical upheavals that have shaken the roots of Jewish existence.

The difference between Mr. Heilprin and his ancestors is irrelevant to Kafka's world. The ignorance of the law, for him, is inherent in the very idea of law, not the result of a process in time. The existence of authority, the "nobility," necessarily implies, according to "The Problem of Our Laws" (*CS* 437–38), that the laws entrusted into their hands are secret. To know them would undermine their absolute authority. That is why the nobility would vanish once "everything became clear." But we cannot *want* them to vanish, for they are "the sole visible and indubitable law that is imposed upon us." Therefore, no law can ever become clear.

Thus, the only indubitable law is authority and its arbitrary acts. It is binding *because* it is arbitrary, because it is inexplicable. Its inexplicability is inherent in it and gives the law absolute validity by exempting it from all dependence on external reasons. *Loi* and *récit* (or *histoire*, or *genèse*, or *dérivation*) must exclude one another, as Derrida puts it in "Devant la Loi."[20] History and historical change are therefore indifferent as far as the ignorance of the law is concerned. Rather, one could say with Walter Benjamin that Kafka brings us back to a prehistoric world in which laws remain unwritten. *The Trial,* says Benjamin, "takes us back far beyond the time of the giving of the Law on twelve tablets to a prehistoric world, written law being one of the first victories scored over this world. In Kafka the written law is contained in books, but these are secret; by basing itself on them the prehistoric world exerts its rule all the more ruthlessly."[21] Prehistoric forces, that is, "may justifiably be regarded as belonging to our world as well."[22] The history that comes between makes little difference.

IV   For Agnon it makes all the difference. It is an object for lament, but also, perhaps, reason for some hope. For if the separation from the law is historical process, not metaphysical necessity, the law may be recoverable. It may be undecipherable rather than lost.[23]

The existence of a known law, though largely abandoned, forms a firm, objective background against which individual failure can be diagnosed. The inaccessibility of the law in Kafka, on the other hand, makes the distinction between general and individual, outer and inner, objective and subjective, quite impossible. The two writers' treatment of time is a case in point. In "The Book of Deeds" one is always late, missing buses, trains, meetings. One's personal time keeps clashing with an impersonal time that ignores one's difficulty in conforming to it.[24] In Kafka, though his heroes also keep missing things, there is no clear-cut distinction between their time and external time because the latter has lost its independent, objective standing. Outer time has been relativized and can no longer serve as a firm yardstick for our failings. Instead, it cruelly returns to us the image of our own infirmities. The glaring example is "A Common Confusion" (*CS* 429–30).

More generally, the Kafkaesque confusion between projection and reality, though seemingly part of the fantastic in "The Book of Deeds," in fact stops short in Agnon of the fantastic proper. "Abandon" can serve again as a good example. To the narrator walking in the dark alley, the heavy shadows first *seem* like a wall, then actually become one when he considers going to the end of the road to check whether there is an opening in the wall. A projection of his anguished mind materializes into solid reality. At first sight this is no different from the joiner Lanz episode in *The Trial,* when K. comes to an apartment where the man he has "invented" actually lives. Unlike K., however, Agnon's narrator is perfectly aware that this is illusion. "I knew they were only shadows," he says, "but they seemed like a wall." Or again, "When one is in a hurry and there is only one bus, every shadow becomes a wall." The confusion between reality and the projections of the mind is psychologically motivated, and the *merveilleux* dissolves into *l'étrange,* just as the tomblike room and the grotesque judge will later dissolve into the narrator's mental setup.

V   One could say, therefore, that the supernatural, indispensable in Kafka, is dispensable in Agnon. For in Kafka it is the only possible representation of the inexplicable, while in Agnon it is one possible metaphor for a crisis. In Kafka its incomprehensibility is part of what it stands for; in Agnon it was preceded, and will be superseded by the comprehensible.

The comprehensible, of course, is the Torah. In many "Books of Deeds" stories the Torah is debased or abandoned. The path to salvation seems blocked, and the narrative ends in a cul-de-sac. If, in the final analysis, the cul-de-sac is ambivalent, this is because Agnon sends us one message through his narrative, another through his language.

"Abandon" will again show what I mean. The story, as we know by now, is about being away from home, missing the way back, and being put on trial instead. This Kafka-like plot differs from Kafka, we have seen, in that it rationalizes away its supernatural element by defining the guilt that "produces" the trial. The emphasis is on defining, for the sense of guilt itself exists in *The Trial* as well. In "Abandon," however, the guilt is clearly defined as self-centeredness and alienation from religion and people.

If the definition of guilt gives moral and religious intelligibility to the story and shows its supernatural, that is, unintelligible, elements to be dispensable, the predicament described may be real enough. The narrator *has* drifted far away from home, people, and religion, and is now facing the void. Or has he, and is he? The narrator's voice, as distinct from his story, is steeped in the doctrine whose loss he is lamenting.

Take the first sentence of the story. The days on which the narrator and Heilprin meet at the café are days "devoid of pleasure." The idiom used in the original Hebrew refers the reader to Ecclesiastes 12:1, which describes the evil days of old age,[25] but it also refers him, less neutrally, to several other verses in the Bible, for instance Hosea 8:8 ("Now shall they be among the Gentiles as a vessel wherein is no pleasure"), which describes the punishment of Israel for having forgotten their Maker. In the next sentence Mr. Heilprin is described as "highborn." The Hebrew "Ben Gedolim" (literally, "child of mighty ones") refers the learned reader to a place in the Talmud where Ben Gedolim is contrasted with "Ben Torah" (child of the Torah). Ben Gedolim thus implies a value judgment and means "highborn, but deficient in learning and spiritual stature."

In the same sentence the distinguished families from which Heilprin is descended are said to have "sustained us during our long exile and given us power to stand among the nations." Two references are implied here.

First, the Hebrew for "sustained us" is an idiom that strongly evokes a verse from the Passover *Haggadah:* "And that promise [God's to Israel] has sustained our fathers and ourselves, for not one persecutor only has risen against us to destroy us; but in every generation there are those who rise against us to destroy us. But the Holy One always saves us from their hands." Thus, what really "sustained us during our long exile" is our faith in God and his miraculous aid. The idiom used, "amdu lanu," moreover, is repeated later on, when the narrator notices someone following him and decides he cannot help him: "I could not sustain him in his need." There is a clear reference here to the Mishna (Avot 2:3): "appearing as friends when it is to their own advantage, they sustain not a man in the hour of his need." The moral nature of the narrator's conduct is here implied: he is one of those who appear as friends when it is to their own advantage, but do not stand by a man in the hour of his need. The verbal connection with "sustained us during our long exile" sets off the contrast between the high moral standards of old times and the opportunistic cynicism of the present.

Second, "given us power to stand" is an equally strong reference to "ye shall have no power to stand before your enemies" (Leviticus 26:37), part of an angry warning to Israel to keep God's commandments.

Finally, in the last sentence of the first paragraph, one's soul is said to "weep in secret for the pride of Israel." These words refer to Jeremiah 13:17: "But if ye will not hear it, my soul shall weep in secret places for your pride." "Pride" (an unusual Hebrew form is used here) can refer to a greatness gone, as in Agnon. But it can also refer to the arrogance that has made Israel ignore God's word, as from two verses earlier in Jeremiah: "Hear ye, and give ear; be not proud: for the Lord hath spoken." Thus, the biblical reference adds a second, hidden sense to Agnon's words: One's soul weeps both for the fall of Israel and for their atheistic arrogance.

The story's first paragraph alone (unusually rich, one must admit, in biblical and talmudic connotations), has provided us with five instances of implicit reference to the doctrine whose decline is the theme of the story. In all five cases the reference is to the dangers of and punishment for neglecting God's word; so far, these connotations support the theme. But the very fact that the narrator's language can, and is intended to, evoke such associations shows that he is addressing a narratee who can appreciate it. The narratee, unlike Mr. Heilprin, is Ben Torah, if not necessarily Ben Gedolim. His contract with the narrator includes the knowledge of Bible and Gemara, not at all in line with their neglect, with the "hefker" the story describes. Thus, the narrator's language keeps refuting his message. It keeps declaring the potency of the doctrine whose death it laments.

There is no better example of this than the description of the grotesque judge in the last part of the story. I have mentioned the oxymora used there: he is neither young nor old, his mustache is both white and black, his hat is both cantor's hat and a hat of the secret police. The Israeli critic Gershon Shaked has shown these to be parodistic references to the oxymora describing God in the Shir

Hakavod (hymn of glory) included in the Sabbath service:[26] "They
saw in thee both age and youth. . . . He hath bound a helmet of
victory upon his head." Parody, of course, depends on a knowledge
of the text parodied. In this case the ridiculous judge, by referring us
to the Shir Hakavod, asserts the God that he negates. God, like
objective time mentioned earlier, is the firm yardstick by which
human failings are measured and condemned.

Kafka's Bürgel, on the other hand, or Klamm for that matter,
is a parody with no definite text parodied. He too has "a certain
contradictoriness": the chubby cheeks and merry eyes of a child
and the high forehead, narrow mouth, and pointed nose that show
superior intellect. But this contradictoriness, though perhaps very
generally referring to the oxymoric technique of theological and
mystical writings, betrays no specific origin, asserts no specific
God.

This is typical of Kafka's language as a whole: lucid, neutral,
hardly ever thickened by intertextual connotations. His is a language diametrically opposed to a language such as Agnon's, which
constantly evokes a doctrine. The world emptied of a doctrine is
duplicated in a language emptied of associations. The tautological,
only possible, message is couched in words that refer to nothing
beyond themselves. "The incomprehensible is incomprehensible,
and we know that already."

One wonders how far this difference between the two writers,
and perhaps not only this one, has to do with the language they
chose to write in. Both were Jews, both were born in the 1880s in
provinces of the Austro-Hungarian Empire. But whereas Kafka
wrote in German, Agnon wrote for a while in Yiddish but mainly
in Hebrew. That is, Kafka wrote in a language that, though the
language of Western culture in Prague, belonged neither to the
Jews nor to the Czechs. In a diary entry for October 24, 1911, he
writes about its "Christian coldness," its distance from Jewish
emotions:

> Yesterday it occurred to me that I did not always love my
> mother as she deserved and as I could, only because the Ger-
> man language prevented it. The Jewish mother is no "Mutter,"

to call her "Mutter" makes her a little comic (not to herself, because we are in Germany), we give a Jewish woman the name of a German mother, but forget the contradiction that sinks into the emotions so much the more heavily, "Mutter" is peculiarly German for the Jew, it unconsciously contains, together with the Christian splendour Christian coldness also, the Jewish woman who is called "Mutter" therefore becomes not only comic but strange. Mama would be a better name if only one didn't imagine "Mutter" behind it. I believe that it is only the memories of the ghetto that still preserve the Jewish family, for the word "Vater" too is far from meaning the Jewish father. (*D* 88)

But wasn't it precisely this "coldness" that made German an ideal medium for an experience such as Kafka's? And weren't Yiddish and Hebrew, intimately associated with Jewish life and history, Agnon's natural tool? When he tried in "The Book of Deeds" to apply Hebrew to a Kafkaesque experience, it refused him. The emptiness he meant it to express came alive with the many echoes of a living tradition.

9

Comrade Kafka: Antifascist Fairy Tales of the Thirties

I   "We find in him," Brecht once wrote of Kafka, "strange disguises prefiguring many things that were, at the same time when his books appeared, plain to very few people. The fascist dictatorship was, so to speak, in the very bones of the bourgeois democracies, and Kafka described with wonderful imaginative power the future concentration camps, the future instability of the law, the future absolutism of the state *apparat,* the paralysed, inadequately motivated, floundering lives of the many individual people; everything appeared as in a nightmare and with the confusion and inadequacy of nightmare."[1]

Reality as nightmare was increasingly the way the world appeared to writers and readers when Kafka's works, translated by Willa and Edwin Muir, were appearing in England one by one: *The Castle* in 1930, *The Great Wall of China* in 1933, *The Trial* in 1937, and *America* in 1938.[2] The impersonal, dictatorial force that informed the world of a writer who had died ten years before seemed to be materializing before their very eyes. His own country was soon to become the first victim of that brutal force.

Not that the political implications—or possibilities of application—of Kafka's work were necessarily foremost in the minds of his first English readers. They were certainly far from the mind of Edwin Muir himself, who was above all fascinated by the spiritual and mystical import of Kafka's work, so peculiarly coupled with concreteness and solidity.[3] The mystical is the timeless, and Muir's preoccupation with Jungian archetypes was ahistorical and diametrically opposed to the subordination of literature to the topical. Kafka, to him, was the very archetype of the archetypal: "In an age obsessed by the time sense, or, as it is called, the historical sense, [Kafka] has resurrected and made available for contemporary use the timeless story, the archetypal story, in which is the source of all stories."[4]

To Muir's Marxist contemporaries this ahistoricism was anathema. They *were* "obsessed by the time sense." The communist novelist Edward Upward ridiculed the Jungian concept of literature in a "Sketch for a Marxist Interpretation of Literature" published in 1937: "To suppose that literature reflects nothing at all, or that, as Jung supposes, it reflects archetypal images which exist quite independently of the material world, is to suppose that a writer can think without using his material brain."[5] It was only natural that Upward should object to the association of his own work with the "archetypal" Kafka. He congratulated a research student on noticing that his novel *Journey to the Border* (1938) was not at all Kafkaesque: "Insofar as it is influenced by Kafka at all—and I had read *The Castle* before I started writing *Journey to the Border*—I would say that it is an anti-Kafkaesque novel. Its 'message' obviously is 'Stop being fantastic, stop being like Kafka's K., stop searching about within your soul for a solution of your problems and start trying to find a solution by means of action in the external world!'"[6] Upward was quite right. *Journey to the Border,* which describes a day in the life of a hired tutor who finally realizes that he "must get in touch with the workers' movement,"[7] is anything but Kafkaesque. The fact that both Spender, C. Day Lewis, and Muir thought it was[8] only shows that any use of extended symbolism[9] plus a considerable amount of anguish was likely to be associated with Kafka in the minds of the English in the 1930s.

Kafka, to the Marxist Upward, was fantastic and introvert; literature had to be realistic and extrovert. But Kafka's introspective fantasies, the Marxists felt, had the power to evoke a communal nightmare beyond his own. That is why he could be revised to express what he perhaps had no intention of expressing. That is why he was both embraced and rejected by the English Left in the thirties.

He was embraced because, as Brecht later put it in the lines I have quoted, all the ailments of the bourgeois democracies had been, as it were, diagnosed in his work: congenital fascism, precariousness of the law, absolutism of the state. He was rejected because he had not drawn the necessary conclusions, had not attained the "goal."[10] But there was an openness about him, a refusal to commit himself to any system of symbols existing in the real world,[11] which, though reactionary from the Marxist point of view, could be made politically useful:

> Kafka's influence . . . [sprang] also from the evident possibility of applying his symbolism to the social situation. Malraux and Hemingway had been able to say something directly about the social and moral problems of the time without using symbolism or descending to propaganda, but this direct approach was (as it seemed) possible because they were both men of action. The symbolism of Kafka offered another strategy to those who were not eager participants in warfare. The artists might tell the truth of our times symbolically or in parable. I remember going round, after first reading Kafka, telling my friends that his apparatus of ambiguity could be used for all sorts of purposes, comic, tragic or merely mysterious, and that *such a technique might produce anti-Fascist fairy tales of great power and beauty.*[12]

II   Rex Warner and Ruthven Todd may or may not have been two of the friends to whom Julian Symons told this. Both, at all events, used Kafka to produce "anti-Fascist fairy tales." I don't think any of the four novels I shall consider here, two by each, is successful. They are often tedious, blatantly didactic, and marred by arbitrary and excessive Kafkaisms. Except for *The Aerodrome* they have been largely forgotten, and rightly so. Interestingly, however, the English novelists' misreading of Kafka, though reductive and often naïve, is subtler than meets the eye. Particularly Ruthven Todd seems to show an early insight into what Kafka's work is all about. Kafka's agnosticism did not, in the final analysis, let the two writers turn him into a political ideologist.

The novels in question are *The Wild Goose Chase* (1937) and *The*

Aerodrome (1941), by Rex Warner, and *Over the Mountain* (1939) and *The Lost Traveller* (1943), by Ruthven Todd. The dominant Kafkan influence on all four is *The Castle,* though *The Trial,* too, looms large. This is already evident from the journey and quest imagery implied in all four titles, which is also central to *The Castle.*[13] The particular influence of *The Castle* may have to do with the fact that this was the first work by Kafka to be published in English and hence, perhaps, had greater impact than the rest. It may also be accounted for by the fact that K. of *The Castle,* unlike Joseph K. of *The Trial* or Samsa of "The Metamorphosis," must have struck the radical reader as an active fighter for a better world, a prototype of the social revolutionary. That is how a later Marxist critic, the Czech Jiři Hájek, puts it:

> The Surveyor K., the central figure of Kafka's last novel, *The Castle,* seeks an escape from the labyrinth of the reified, alienated world, into which Joseph K., Gregor Samsa, and the majority of Kafka's "heroes" have been exiled. He seeks an escape by trying to join the collective of the Castle's subjects, in order to serve them with his work . . . the difference between the surveyor and all of Kafka's previous heroes [is that] he takes up the struggle to change his fate not from compulsion, but through his own decision. Probably he is indeed the only hero full of activity and the longing for socially useful deeds.[14]

In the sentence, "He seeks an escape by trying to join the collective of the Castle's subjects, in order to serve them with his work," one notices the leftist predilection for village over castle, subjects over master, collective over individual struggle. This, as we shall see, applies to Rex Warner's reading of *The Castle* as well. It is a reading that can be traced back to Max Brod's postscript to the first German edition of the novel (1926), except that Brod had regarded integration into the life of the "collective" as a religious rather than social achievement, a way of connecting with the Castle which, to him, meant divine grace.[15] Here is how Muir, who follows him, puts it:

> The problem with which all Kafka's work is concerned is a moral and spiritual one. It is a twofold problem: that of find-

ing one's true vocation, one's true place, whatever it may be, in the community; and that of acting in accordance with the will of heavenly powers. But though it has those two aspects it was in his eyes a single problem; for a man's true place in the community is finally determined not by secular, but by divine, law. And only when, by apparent chance or deliberate effort, a man finds himself in his divinely appointed place, can he live as he should.[16]

The Marxist reading isolates, so to speak, the community aspect from the divine law aspect, the social from the metaphysical, and makes it self-sufficient: one must join the collective "in order to serve them with his work." But what about the opposite pole, that of the Castle itself? What place does the Castle occupy within the antifascist allegory our English novelists model on *The Castle*?

It is a measure of the derivative, weak quality of all four novels that what they borrow from their strong precursor is not only the duality itself of village versus Castle, but the very details of the Castle's physical appearance. If the Castle hill first appears to K. "veiled in mist and darkness," (*C* 9) the "Pale Peak," which nobody ever crossed and which Michael, the narrator of Todd's *Over the Mountain*, crosses (or rather thinks he crosses), is surrounded by "swirling yellow mist."[17] More significant, because less obviously symbolic, is the second appearance of the Castle to K., echoed both in the two Rex Warner novels and in Todd's other novel, *The Lost Traveller*:

The Castle:

It was . . . a rambling pile consisting of innumerable small buildings closely packed together and of one or two storeys; if K. had not known that it was a castle he might have taken it for a little town. There was only one tower as far as he could see, whether it belonged to a dwelling-house or a church he could not determine. Swarms of crows were circling round it.

. . . it was after all only a wretched-looking town, a huddle of village houses . . . the plaster had long since flaked off and the stone seemed to be crumbling away. . . . The tower above him here—the only one visible—the tower of a house, as was now apparent, perhaps of the main building, was uniformly round, part of it graciously mantled with ivy, pierced by small windows that glittered in the sun, a somewhat maniacal glitter, and topped by what looked like an attic, with battlements that were irregular, broken, fumbling, as if designed by the trembling or careless hand of a child, clearly outlined against the blue. (*C* 15–16)

The Wild Goose Chase:

It was a long building of two storeys high and must once have been handsome, though now the roof needed repair, the paint on the windows was peeling, and of the outhouses which surrounded the courtyard many were in a state of collapse. It was surprising to . . . find the farm so dilapidated, with tiles off the roof, glass out of windows. But, for all that, the building was a pleasant sight glowing red in the setting sun . . . overhead rooks flapped cawing black to tree tops.[18]

The Aerodrome:

. . . the aerodrome on the summit of the hill. . . . The long hangars were set not in rows nor in any regular order, but were so disposed and camouflaged that even from quite close at hand they appeared merely as rather curious modifications of the natural contours of our hills. . . . Many of these buildings also, where visible, resembled older landmarks. One of the main depots for the storage of arms had been constructed so as to appear indistinguishable from a country church; the canteen . . . resembled, in spite of the luxury within, an old barn. . . .

. . . I paused at the bottom of the fields below the aerodrome, looking uphill to the tin hut. . . . The late afternoon sun glistened from its roof, so that in the landscape it appeared an object of special importance as to me it was certainly more important than any other building; and as I noted its distance it seemed to me a jewel, minute and inestimable.[19]

The Lost Traveller

That [i.e., the city at sundown the day before] had been an affair of concrete buildings that resembled boxes . . . while this was a most peculiar mixture of all sorts of Gothic and baroque revival architecture, arranged in the most higgedly-piggedly manner imaginable.

It was built of red and yellow brick, crowned with useless things, stone eagles perched on the top of minute villas, an electric power station, or some such building, possessed a chimney which was the replica of a cathedral tower, complete to the elaborate carving and the gargoyles . . . each of the pinnacles on the chimney was as sharp and clear as if engraved against the sky.[20]

These descriptions quoted here as analogous to Kafka's description of the Castle are not descriptions of a castle—neither Warner nor Todd goes *that* far—but of places that are its structural counterparts; that is, are at the opposite pole to (though not always furthest from) the hero's home town: a farm beyond the frontier in *Wild Goose Chase,* the aerodrome and a nearby hut in *Aerodrome,* the fantastic city the traveler reaches in *Lost Traveller.* Though they are different places—farm, aerodrome, city—they all share certain components of the Kafka description. They have a squat, crouching shape (all three), irregular (*A, LT*), old, peeling, crumbling (*WGC, A*); they have a tower associated with a church tower (*A, LT*), and they glitter in the sun or are clearly outlined against a blue sky (all three). In one case (*WGC*) Kafka's crows are circling overhead.

These recurring elements seem to fall under two headings: shabbiness and decline on the one hand, celestiality and radiance on the other. Although what could be a church proves, as in Kafka, not so—it is a depot in *The Aerodrome,* a power station in *The Lost Traveller*—it is still associated with a church and thus is lent spiritual, or mock-spiritual significance. The way the buildings glow red, or glisten in the sun, or are engraved against the sky enhances their mystical character. At the same time, however, they are low-lying, dilapidated, and in a state of collapse.

In Kafka this oxymoron, informing as it does the entire novel with its twofold image of the Castle as both infinitely desirable and sordid, has produced different interpretations, reinforcing the view that Kafka is essentially unreadable, irreducible to definite meanings. As early as in his postscript to the first edition, Brod had to enlist Kierkegaard to reconcile his equation of the Castle and divine grace with the Sortini episode, in which a Castle official requires the village girl Amalia to do something "obviously immoral and sordid."[21] Brod ingeniously interpreted this paradox of immoral Providence as an assertion of Kierkegaard's claim that "the categories of morality and religion are by no means to be seen as overlapping."[22] Erich Heller, shocked by Brod's "unfathomable depths of nonsense," opted for the other term of the oxymoron: "the castle represents neither divine guidance or Heaven," it is "the heavily fortified garrison of a company of Gnostic demons"; it is for K. "something that is to be conquered, something that bars his way into a purer realm."[23] There is a third way: integrating the two terms of the oxymoron into an *acte gratuit*. This is Camus's way. To Camus, as we have seen, Kafka deifies the absurd by "recapturing God through what negates him," by recognizing him, "not according to our categories of goodness and beauty, but behind the empty and hideous aspects of his indifference, of his injustice, and of his hatred." The land surveyor, to Camus, forsakes morality, logic, and intellectual truths "in order to enter, endowed solely with his mad hope, the desert of divine grace." He "embraces the God that consumes him"—a Kierkegaardian act of which Camus disapproves.

III   This *acte gratuit* is definitely not what our four heroes have in mind. Nor do they embrace their respective "castles" as the ultimate good. Both Rex Warner and Ruthven Todd, miswriting *The Castle* to produce antifascist fables, naturally turn the Castle itself into a bulwark of corrupt absolutism that must be destroyed, as in Erich Heller's reading, except that the "purer realm" to which its destruction should lead is that of socialism. Dualism here is Marxist, not gnostic, with Count West-West—or Klamm—playing the part of the capitalist demiurge, and K. joining the "collective" to defeat him and reach the real good beyond him. This equation of the Castle with social evil means that all four heroes must wish not to be accepted by the Castle, as in Kafka, but to destroy it. George in *Wild Goose Chase,* Roy in *Aerodrome,* Michael in *Over the Mountain,* and Christopher in *The Lost Traveller* all either hope to see their "castle" destroyed or actually destroy it.

At this point, a short outline of the four novels seems to be called for. Acquaintance with them, after all, cannot be taken for granted.

George, hero of Warner's *The Wild Goose Chase,* is one of three brothers who leave their seaside town on a journey beyond the frontier to chase the Wild Goose. Both the motive of the quest and the nature of its object are unclear. Years later, George comes back and tells his story, which constitutes the bulk of the novel. It is divided into two parts, entitled "The One Remains" and "The Many Change," corresponding to George's initial individualism and his later realization that it is only "by taking his place in the inevitable movement of the mass" (*WGC* 236) that he can achieve his end. Being present, after crossing the frontier, at a revolutionary assembly of farmers, slaves to the town and its governing hierarchy of secret agents, policemen, and, at the top "men of science, politicians, and ministers of religion capable of exerting terrific power" (*WGC* 116), George is disillusioned with the farmers' apathy and goes to town, a science fiction city, complete with artificial lighting, motor bicycle tracks on roofs, and chemical food in tablet form. There he is arrested for a crime whose nature he doesn't know, has an audition with a royal hierarchy of three kings, escapes back to the countryside, rejects his own "individual escapade" (here part 2 begins), regains the farmers' confidence, and creates the "revolutionary army of peasants and workers" (*WGC* 306), which finally conquers the town and rips open its roofs to allow the warm sunlight in. Is the new government likely to become as tyrannical as the old one? Or will it permit the chase of the bird and encourage "the disinterested work of the spirit" (*WGC* 403)? When George makes his final speech—"we are on the way to create a new civilization" (*WGC* 440)—a horde of huge white birds flies across the sky.

Roy, in Warner's other novel, *The Aerodrome,* lives in a village opposite a well-camouflaged air base, on whose premises no unauthorized villager is allowed. The airmen are handsome, immensely wealthy, respected, and envied by the villagers. The cohesion of village life, the absolute authority of squire and parson, are threatened by the aerodrome, and the visiting Air Vice-Marshall declares that the village is to be taken over by the Air Force. It actually is, with everything natural and traditional (trees) replaced by the artificial and mechanized (ashtrays). While Roy enlists, gets to the aerodrome and seems to be converted to its totalitarian weltanschauung, his friend the Flight Lieutenant, who is given a job in the village, is undergoing the opposite transformation and becomes a fanatic villager. Freedom from time, from parents, possessions, history, love, emotion, shapelessness; a new mastery of the self and "freedom through the recognition of necessity," discipline for the sake of power, and power for the sake of freedom (*A* 118–19) is the Air Vice-Marshall's credo. His is not just an air base, but "an organization manifestly entitled by its own discipline, efficiency and will to assume supreme power" (*A* 143) and dominate the world. Roy finally realizes that the Air Force has destroyed "the sweet and terrifying sympathy of love that can acknowledge mystery, danger and dependence" and has erected a "barren edifice of perfection," a creed of the "denial of life" (*A* 166, 169, 180). After a melodramatic series of stunning discoveries (both Roy and the Flight Lieutenant turn out to be the Air Vice-Marshall's sons), the "new order" collapses and Roy is back to his first love, Bess.

Michael, narrator of Ruthven Todd's *Over the Mountain,* longs to cross the "Pale Peak" overlooking his home town. Many have tried but nobody has yet succeeded in doing so. It isn't "the mere pimple on the earth's surface" that attracts Michael, but the "unknown country" on the other side of the mountain (*OM* 18). After an awesome struggle with winds and snowstorms, he arrives, weather-beaten and amnesic, at the other side, where everything— meddlesome journalists, hypocritical church, all-mighty police—is familiar, except that it is worse, more dictatorial, more absolutist. Michael joins a revolutionary movement, inadvertently kills the head of the Secret Service, escapes, knows he "would be branded as a Red by the prosecutor" (*OM* 156), hears of concentration camps and torture, realizes that in this "damned queer country" he must be viewed as an "eccentric" clinging to the "heresy" that "all men were created equal" (*OM* 181). Climbing the peak to flee back to his own democracy, he is defeated by the snow, must return to the fascist side, and then, in a final shock of recognition, discovers he has never left his own country, never crossed the Pale Peak.

Finally, Christopher Aukland of *The Lost Traveller* is harmlessly window-shopping down the street when he hears an explosion and finds himself in an incomprehensibly timeless desert. Passing through a gully in a ridge back to time's region, he comes to a seemingly empty, surreal city, with bleeding bronze statues and a mysterious, invisible "He" whose word is law. Christopher is arrested, hopes to get in touch with his consul and get an interim passport to return home, but is refused and cannot speak to "Him," who is unreachable. One can only speak to Omar, his chief liaison officer. Omar is at the top of the town hierarchy; second come the officials, and third the simple citizens, who are faceless, "merely eyes and holes for nostrils and mouths" (*LT* 60), and called by initials only. Christopher would like to consult law books, but nobody in this country "ever pleads not guilty" (*LT* 93). Besides, he has no idea what his crime is. To make the punishment fit the criminal, Omar sentences *Auk*land to hunt the great *auk*. Since this sea bird is extinct, this is "as hopeless a venture as he could imagine" (*LT* 118). His boat sunk, he finds himself in a hut, and when one of the men around him lifts his hand to hit him with a bludgeon, he glances down at his own body and sees he is a bird. The hunt for the great auk has come to nothing; *he* is the last great auk.

IV   All four protagonists, to take up our last point, view the "castle" as evil incarnate and want it destroyed. George conquers the capitalist town with his revolutionary army; Roy, though seduced for a while by the Air Vice-Marshall's creed of pseudofreedom, comes to see that it stands for the denial of life and witnesses its self-destruction; Michael, though his castle, to invert the phrase, turns out to be his own house, discovers its fascist nature and wishes its overthrow; and the surreal city to which Christopher roams is a place of injustice and tyranny.

Hence, although the above descriptions all follow Kafka's paradoxical portrayal of the Castle as both spiritual and seedy, they do not do so in order to lend ambiguity to their "castles." There is nothing ambiguous about the English novelists' concept of a declining regime marked out for destruction. If nevertheless they describe these doomed places as glittering in the sun, or associate them with a church, they do so not to put them in an ambiguous light but, among other reasons, to ironize them or show their false seductivity. As so often with Kafka's descendants, his infinitely resonant symbols are miswritten as flat signs.

In Rex Warner's case the distinction between resonant symbol and flat sign is a conscious one. In an essay entitled "The Allegorical Method" he distinguishes the "overt" allegory of a Bunyan or a Swift from the "occult" one of Melville, Dostoyevsky, or Kafka. The former is meant "to give vigor and vividness to a definite belief," the latter "to attempt fantastically to throw some light on what is beyond the ordinary reach of words."[24] Where would Warner place himself? He has been called the English Kafka,[25] but he is clearly an "overt" allegorist. Rather than "groping towards a meaning that cannot be perfectly expressed,"[26] he seems to have an a priori, well-defined belief. Every critic who has compared him with Kafka has, indeed, insisted on precisely this difference between the two: "Kafka's allegory creates an experience whereas Warner's merely reproduces."[27]

I agree, and yet *The Wild Goose Chase* demonstrates that its author had some inhibitions about politicizing his Kafka. He was aware, it seems, not only of Kafka's potentialities for political allegory, but also of his resistance to definite messages. His allegory, therefore, although it does clearly "reproduce" a definite belief, also suggests a groping toward something else.

The definite political patterns—proletariat versus capitalist, individualist "freethinking" versus mass movement—are conveyed through George's story and determine the overall structure of the novel. Kafkaesque motifs are revised to enhance the political message. Thus, the suspicious, apathetic nature of the villagers of *The Castle* becomes the proletarians' indifference to revolutionary activity; the Castle officials' use of Amalia or Frieda becomes frequent rapes of country girls by policemen (*WGC* 116); the mysterious laughter of the policeman in Kafka's short piece "Give It Up!" (*CS* 456), or the warder's guffaw at the beginning of *The Trial* (*T* 7), becomes brutal laughter that repeats ad nauseam whenever George encounters a policeman (*WGC* 103 and passim); the legal hierarchy of *The Trial* becomes the state hierarchy (*WGC* 116), and Joseph K.'s irregular arrest is repeated in George's case (*WGC* 212–13). Above all, K.'s insistence on becoming a citizen of the village as a means of getting to the Castle is transformed into George's option for the mass movement rather than the "individual method." Other Kafkaesque elements applied to this portrait of fascism seem less applicable: the distribution of obscene photographs by the fascist government (*WGC* 119) (a replica of the indecent pictures in the law books in *The Trial* [*T* 60–61]), or the audition George has with the Headmaster, where he is strangely not allowed to see him (invisible Count West-West?) and instead receives his answers on typewritten sheets pushed beneath a curtain (*WGC* 175–76). Here, one feels, the Kafka imitation becomes utterly mechanical.

But the political countryside-versus-town duality is put in the framework of a larger duality: George's seaside town, from which he sets out on his quest, versus the wild goose, which is the object of his quest. The political duality seems to be transcended by this larger duality, which calls for definition.

The first pole of this larger duality, the seaside town of the prologuelike first two chapters (*WGC* 15–36), is once again heavily Kafkaesque. The "sobriety" of its architecture, its "church's straight brown spire" (*WGC* 16), cannot fail to remind the reader of K.'s native town with its church tower, "firm in line, soaring unfalteringly to its tapering point," an "earthly building," but with "a clearer meaning than the muddle of everyday life" (*C* 15). And if this clear, earthly meaning of the church of K.'s native town is contrasted with the "maniacal glitter" of the Castle tower, the sobriety of George's place is similarly contrasted with the "supernatural" helter-skeltering of the gulls over the cliff face, and with the brothers' "dubious" quest, whose motives or object remain unexplained (*WGC* 16, 28). The religious nature of the contrast is throughout suggested by the Prebendary's contempt for the undertaking, the slap in the face he gets from George, apparently for no good reason, and the mystical references to geese and birds, including Leda's divine swan (*WGC* 30). The birdlike imprint of a webbed foot on the belly of George's mother (*WGC* 29) is reminiscent, of course, of Leni's webbed hand in *The Trial* (*T* 123).

George's quest, then, is mystically motivated, and its object, as indicated by the very title of the novel, is ever elusive. "A pursuit of something as unlikely to be caught as the wild goose" is how Dr. Johnson defines "wild goose chase" in his *Dictionary*. The "something" that is pursued is not the workers' government that is set up at the end of the novel. The wild geese, whenever George sees and hears them, combine the celestial music of Kafka's Castle ("a clear musical note of an overpowering sweetness," *WGC* 100) with, perhaps, elements from Yeats's "Leda and the Swan" ("a rushing of wings beating up furiously the air," *WGC* 99) and even Hopkins's "The Windhover" ("the power of the thing," *WGC* 100). They have, in other words, various religious connotations, though not in the institutionalized sense, and are expressly different from any social end. Indeed, on completing the revolution George says: "I am uniquely interested in chasing the wild goose. This revolution, these ambitious schemes of reorganization, I have worked hard for them, as I work for my bread, because they have been necessary things. But like bread they are only means to an end, and, important as they are, they are no more important to me than a crust of bread when I compare them with my ultimate object" (*WGC* 405).

As in Erich Heller's reading of *The Castle*, Rex Warner's "castle" also must be destroyed to get to a "purer realm" beyond it, to George's "ultimate object." This ultimate object, which, according to the novel's political logic should be the socialism that will succeed the dictatorship of the proletariat, remains, according to the novel's imagistic logic, undefinable and unreachable. This seems to be Warner's homage to the true Kafka. Except that in George's final speech this ultimate object *is* defined, and its definition—a puerile mixture of bohemian pose, supercilious (partly Audenesque) wit, and honest emotion—testifies to Warner's, and his generation's, basic confusion: "What our old leaders most respected we chiefly despise—the frantic assertion of an ego, do-nothings, the over-cleanly, deliberate love making, literary critics, moral philosophers, ball room dancing, pictures of sunsets, money, the police; and to what they used to despise we attach great value—to comradeship, and to profane love, to hard work, honesty, the sight of the sun, reverence for those who have helped us, animals, flesh and blood" (*WGC* 440).

It is a far cry from the radical chic à la 1930s to the Comintern; it is a further cry to Kafka. Warner may have felt that Kafka could not be reduced to the "overt" allegory of Marxism, but the "occult" allegory of the wild goose is, in a sense, an even worse abuse. Iron-ically, Kafka's noncommitment to any definite belief is here misused to give an aura of nondogmatism to the author's own definite be-lief. The final kitsch of the horde of white birds flying across the sky shows that muddled thinking must produce bad writing.

V   In *The Wild Goose Chase* Warner has paid homage (or pseudohomage) to Kafka by shedding ambiguous (or pseudoam-biguous) light on his own definite belief: the destruction of fascism is followed by the hopeless pursuit of the wild goose. In *The Aero-drome* ambiguity appears in another garb: the destruction of the fascist aerodrome is accompanied by the hero's discovery that its führer, the Air Vice-Marshall, is his own father and, moreover, "the impulses of my mind had been the same as his. Now I had found my parents and I had found that I was both united and at variance with them both. In so doing I had also found myself" (*A* 192).

One must own, that is, the fascist in oneself. If the village is instinct, love, and amorphous emotion; and the aerodrome is heartless discipline, mastery, and willpower; man, supposedly, is both. Thus, although the contrast between village and aerodrome abounds once again in Kafkaesque elements, the aerodrome is dif-ferent both from Kafka's Castle and from Warner's own capitalist city in *Wild Goose Chase*. It is neither transcendent like the Castle, nor to be destroyed and transcended like the city. Instead, it is immanent in man.

The contrast between instinctual village and imperious aerodrome derives from *The Castle*. "I was disgusted and frightened," says Roy, "by the contrast between [the villagers'] quick anger, their sudden levity, and the undeviating precision and resolution of the Air Vice-Marshall" (*A* 64–65). One is reminded of the dignified, law-abiding servants up in the Castle, transformed into a "wild unmanageable lot, ruled by their insatiable impulses" in the village (*C* 207). On the other hand, as in Kafka and in Warner's previous novel, the aerodrome shows sexual interest in the village (not to speak of the village girls' attraction to it), and there are "cases of the rape or abduction of young girls carried out by aircraftmen or junior officers" (*A* 10). Other Kafkaesque elements—referable to *The Trial* rather than *The Castle*—are the unawareness of the "real purpose" of the *total* organization,[28] and the "recognition of necessity" the Air Vice-Marshall preaches to the recruits (*A* 118), like the priest to Joseph K. in the cathedral (*T* 243).

But although initially the aerodrome, like the Castle, was unapproachable and "no unauthorized person was allowed on the premises" (*A* 10), it becomes perfectly approachable once Roy joins the Air Force. The entire novel, indeed, unfolds with the progress of this mutuality—both on the part of Roy, who moves toward the aerodrome, and on the part of his friend the Flight Lieutenant, who moves toward the village. When Roy finally witnesses the destruction of the aerodrome, he has symbolically owned it as part of himself.

If the antifascist fairy tale of *Wild Goose Chase* was problematized by means of an open ending, the present tale is problematized through a psychologization of its politics. The political belief remains the same: fascism must be resisted and destroyed. It is the skepticism that takes on a different form. In the earlier novel the question was: What will follow the defeat of fascism? In the later novel it is: Isn't fascism an integral part of man? In both cases skepticism is inspired by Kafka. One cannot take his images and leave his doubts.

VI   The introjection of fascism that we found in *The Aerodrome* is central also to the two novels by Ruthvan Todd. Both end with the sudden discovery that the object of one's quest, either the regime that must be destroyed in *Over the Mountain,* or the bird that must be hunted in *The Lost Traveller,* is none other than oneself: one's own regime, one's own bird body. Although this discovery has obvious political implications, it is above all the futility of the quest that is conveyed through it. The arduous way, it now turns out, has only led back to its starting point, to the quester himself, to his mirror image.

Therefore, although Todd's Kafkaism has been condemned as mechanical and superficial compared to Warner's,[29] I think he shows much insight into what is central to Kafka. Not that the two novels under discussion are commendable in any way. Their imitation is excessive, and they often show grave misunderstanding of what Kafka does, but they do seem to intuit his refusal to regard man's quest as more than mere projection—no small achievement for their time.

The author himself, in "An Attempt at a Preface" to the 1968 reissue of *The Lost Traveller,* strangely regards only the earlier novel, *Over the Mountain,* as Kafkaesque. This, he says, brings it close to *The Wild Goose Chase: "Over the Mountain* was conceived and written before I had read Rex Warner's *The Wild Goose Chase,* and I was, I think, a little chagrined to realize that they were both scions of the same ancestry, and that they both bore some evidence of the political atmosphere of the period of their adolescence" (*LT* 1). The affinity with *Wild Goose Chase* is apparent in the descriptions of the fascist state, its grotesque secret police (the "Blue threads"), and the hero joining the revolutionary underground. Kafka's "ancestry," however, is far more evident in *The Lost Traveller,* published four years later.

It is a sudden explosion that conveys Christopher Aukland, hero of *Lost Traveller,* to the fantastic realm that is this novel's equivalent of the Castle. Or should one say the equivalent of Joseph K.'s arrest, or Samsa's metamorphosis? For the suddenness of the existential upheaval seems to bring it closer to these two works and, of course, to *Alice in Wonderland.* The realm in which Christopher finds himself captive is surreal, and its surreal quality, as in Dali or Magritte, is achieved by a combination of impossible whole and naturalistic detail: the bronze statues that bleed real, sticky blood, or the entrance to the tunnel that vanishes into thin air while the plants now covering it are "real plants, with real sap in their stems, sap which left green and brown stains on his fingers when he squeezed it out" (*LT* 46).

The James Bondian décor—the government offices are all high-speed lifts, moving walls, streamlined armchairs—is anything but Kafkaesque. Despite the combination of the fantastic and the realistic, Todd's descriptions completely lack the natural context in which Kafka embeds the supernatural. Samsa's room, in which the horror of the metamorphosis takes place, is "a regular human bedroom" (*CS* 89). This embedding produces in Kafka the effect of the Freudian "uncanny," the appearance of archaic, primary thinking in the conscious, wide-awake mind. There is nothing of the uncanny about Christopher's adventures in Wonderland. The fantastic context neutralizes the effect of the fantastic occurrences.

Like Samsa, Christopher seeks rational explanations for all the fantastic things he sees. The old man slaughtering the pigeons, Christopher surmises, is "probably engaged in some deep ritual" (*LT* 38); the strange rubber floor must "act as an alarm when he walked" (*LT* 42). "If only he had gone across the flat sands," he sensibly tells himself, like Joseph K., "he would probably have arrived safely at his home" (*LT* 112). Now that he has lost his way, there must be some rational way out: finding his consul, obtaining an interim passport (*LT* 45). But finding the consul is as irrelevant an antidote against existential upheavals as calling a doctor or a plumber in "The Metamorphosis" or wearing a mackintosh in Ionesco's *Amédée*. Unlike Samsa, however, Christopher remains outside the fantasy throughout. He diagnoses it but does not participate in it. He expects his food, for instance, to be "a green veined pill" and is "relieved to find a large plate of bacon" (*LT* 69). He refers to the bird he must hunt as the "*mythical* Great Auk" (*LT* 145). He watches the fantasy but is not himself fantastic, and does not find the fantastic as natural as the dream is to the dreamer.[30] This misunderstanding of Kafka's technique is related to the above one: both by making the entire setting fantastic and by placing Christopher outside it, Todd misses the naturalization of horror that is Kafka's peculiar achievement.

But does he at all try to follow Kafka? Don't the differences outnumber the similarities? They do not. Todd seems to flaunt his Kafkaisms deliberately. Thus, obscene paintings are almost ubiquitous in the town (*LT* 100, 107, 132; cf. *The Trial*); the supreme "He" is invisible and rules by proxy of his officials (*LT* 71; cf. *The Trial*); a renegade movement once tried to claim that "He" had been dead for years (*LT* 72; cf. the "Great Wall of China" fragment); Mali, "a first-grade woman official" joins Christopher in bed and makes love to him (*LT* 68–69; cf. Kafka's whorish women; even the name is reminiscent of Leni of *The Trial*). Christopher has no idea what he is guilty of (*LT* 93; cf. *The Trial*), but no one can ever plead not guilty (*LT* 93, 98; cf. *The Trial*), no one, "of course," can see the legal books (*LT* 92; cf. *The Trial*). Mali uses words that sound like a quotation out of *The Trial:* "If you're guilty, you've no right to appeal, and you're obviously guilty if you've been brought before the court" (*LT* 98). Not only the "logic" of this legal system but all its trappings are pure Kafka: the judge wears "long scarlet robes," his assistants are "soberly clad in black, with top-hats" (*LT* 101). In another part of the novel Kafka's "In the Penal Colony" looms large: Christopher is brought to a "Penal Settlement" (*LT* 120), where inmates are writing "I am a traitor" on the walls (*LT* 125), and one even has the letter *T* (traitor?) branded on his chest (*LT* 127).

VII   *The Lost Traveller* could be dismissed as mindlessly derivative were it not for the interesting turn it takes toward the end. Already when the judge, "[making] the punishment fit the crime and the criminal," sentences Aukland to hunt the great auk (*LT* 108–9), he implicitly identifies the object of the hunt with the hunter. This, too, can be traced back to *The Trial*, but unlike the other borrowed motifs mentioned, this one is far from obvious. It subtly touches on what is central in Kafka. The punishment that fits the crime and the criminal seems to be related to warder Willem's words to Joseph K.:

"Our officials . . . are drawn towards the guilty" (*T* 12). Joseph K.'s inference is that "the Interrogation Chamber must lie in the particular flight of stairs which [he] happened to choose" (*T* 43). This is one of many suggestions in *The Trial* that the arrest and the trial are projections of K.'s guilt—a possibility strongly supported by the joiner Lanz episode (*T* 44–45) but never finally validated. It is a central Kafkaesque motif, intended, I think, not so much to make a positive point about the world as to further our uncertainty about it. Projection is not necessarily the substance of things, but it makes all knowledge of the substance of things impossible. One's self must ever block one's sight.[31]

Christopher Aukland's final quest thus proves doubly futile: both in that the object of his quest is an extinct bird, a wild goose if you wish, and in that it is a projection of himself, he being the hunted bird, finding his own image at the end of the road. The guilt he could not understand is followed by a judgment he cannot understand. Nevertheless, he accepts its necessity and waits, prostrate, for the "stick's inexorable descent" (*LT* 164), much like Joseph K. who, lying on the ground, waits for the butcher's knife to descend, or Samsa who, also transformed into an animal, waits for death.

The replacement of reason by necessity (for example, the priest's caveat to Joseph K. that he must accept things as necessary, not true) is likewise the essence of Father Podmore's teaching in Todd's earlier novel *Over the Mountain*. He speaks to the Narrator Michael of "the necessity of death," "the need for the strong man to wipe the weakling and the hindrance from his path." "It may seem bitter and unjust to you, my son," he adds, "but it is the will of God" (*OM* 199). "My son" will soon prove to be literally true: Father Podmore, the representative of clericalism in the dictatorship on the other side of the mountain, will turn out to be none other than Michael's own father in the so-called democracy on this side of the mountain. The Oedipal flavor enhances the political message: fascism is at one's door. The priest's teaching to Joseph K. is thus politicized, misread as the embodiment of a fascist ideology of suppression. In this sense the novel is political and has a definite message. But at another, more abstract, level, the final discovery that the unknown country on the other side of the mountain is none other than one's own country on this side of the mountain is an admission of the futility of all quests and messages, political or other. It rings in the hollow tautologies of the nursery rhyme that serves as motto to the book:

> A bear went over the mountain,
> A bear went over the mountain,
> A bear went over the mountain
> To see what he could see.
> And what do you think he saw?
> And what do you think he saw?
> The other side of the mountain,
> The other side of the mountain,
> That is all he saw!

At this level Father Podmore's rejection of the human point of view ("it may seem bitter and unjust to you") in the name of necessity ("but it is the will of God")—Brod would say a Kierkegaardian rejection of the ethical for the religious category—is no fascist lore, but despair of knowing. Michael at this level discovers not that his own England is fascist, but that he cannot see beyond his projections. He is as closed in a cabinet of mirrors as is K. in Bürgel's bedroom.

To make such claims for such a poor novel (it tediously draws out Michael's adventures to make the ending the more surprising) seems out of proportion. Insight into a precursor's meaning is no guarantee of success for his follower. If nevertheless I found the four English novels worthy of attention, it is because they show both the potentialities and the limits of the use of Kafka for political writing. Kafka is here misinterpreted as the poet of the nightmare of capitalism, but he keeps reminding his misinterpreters that much more is at stake. His profound agnosticism keeps asserting itself and working against his reduction to definite beliefs. The envisaged social utopia must evaporate into a wild goose chase, and the quest must end in hollow tautology.

I   When Bürgel tells the sleeping K. that he ought to surprise an incompetent secretary in the middle of the night, when he tells him, in other words, that he ought to do what he has just done, he yokes together the greatest promise with the utmost despair. Redemption is anywhere, but it transcends consciousness. The irony of this message can be related to a sentence Kafka never quotes (a sentence meant, admittedly, to make a very different point), the opening sentence of Wittgenstein's *Tractatus Logico-Philosophicus:* "Die Welt ist alles was der Fall ist" (the world is everything that is the case).

Kafka never quotes this sentence. Contemporary American fiction seems fond of it. It appears in John Barth's *The End of the Road* (1958) and looms large, as "the world is all that the case is," in Thomas Pynchon's *V.* (1963).[1] Both novels show a great affinity with Kafka. A third novel I should like to include in my discussion is Kurt Vonnegut, Jr.'s, *Cat's Cradle* (1963). The great differences between the three authors in style, subject matter, and concept of the novel itself show how far-reaching Kafka's influence on modern American fiction is—and how far from obvious. For it has little to do with what we usually call Kafkaesque: offices, corridors, the evils of bureaucracy. It has to do with the deeper level that is my concern in this book.

Above all it has to do with the self-destructive message at the center of Kafka's world. In each of the three American novels, a "doctrine" (or more than one) is offered in answer to a central quest and proves self-canceling. So far they are deeply Kafkaesque. But I shall also try to show that neither Barth, Vonnegut, nor

Pynchon go to the Kafkaesque length of making all thematic extrapolation impossible. Their fictive worlds, each in its own different way, insist on an idea, are relatable to a definable conception of the world. In this they are tamer than their stronger precursor.

In Barth's *The End of the Road*, to take the earliest first,[2] Jake Horner's problem seems the opposite of Kafka's. Rather than being at the bottom of a ravine and thus deprived of the possibility of taking a broad view of matters,[3] he is affiliated with "the malady *cosmopsis,* the cosmic view" (*ER* 73). He is like the proverbial donkey between two piles of straw (*ER* 75), chronically paralyzed by the "recognition of the fact that when one is faced with such a multitude of desirable choices, no one choice seems satisfactory for very long by comparison with the aggregate desirability of all the rest" (*ER* 6). Unlike Kafka's Supplicant in "Description of a Struggle," Jake's problem is not to transcend his perspective, but to have a perspective; not to see things as they are before they show themselves to him, but to see them as they show themselves to *him.* Chameleonlike, he maintains contradictory opinions on any given subject (*ER* 117), has no personality or recognizable self (*ER* 37), cancels himself out, doesn't exist, is nothing (*ER* 66).

What Kafka longed for and found impossible, the broad view of matters, is given to Jake and proves a bane. Instead of revealing an overall law that would give pattern and unity to the gestures of living, it leads to the "void" (*ER* 73) of unlimited choice. Cosmopsis, in its practical results, is no different from the view from the depth of the ravine. "Gazing on eternity, fixed on ultimacy," Jake's "cosmoptic" eyes, "as Winckelmann said inaccurately of the eyes of the Greek statues," are sightless (*ER* 73).

The absence of doctrine in spite of the "cosmic view" turns Jake's existence into what Walter Benjamin calls gestic theater. Gestures lose their obvious fluidity, become deliberate and opaque, a subject, as Benjamin puts it, for reflection without end. Physical self-consciousness produces a typically Kafkaesque combination of first-person narrative and external point of view: "I made a suppositive gesture, which consisted of a slight outward motion of my lapel-grasping left hand, extending simultaneously the fore and index fingers but not releasing my lapel—the hand motion accompanied by quickly arched (and as quickly released) eyebrows, momentarily pursed lips, and an on-the-one-hand/on-the-other-hand rocking of the head" (*ER* 9). This external self-scrutiny goes with Jake's self-image as actor, constantly assigning roles to himself as well as to others, playing games, witnessing shows, wearing masks, capitalizing people into morality-play "essences": The Forty-Year-Old Pickup, The Fresh but Unintelligent Young Man Whose Body One Uses for One's Pleasure without Otherwise Taking Him Seriously (*ER* 29). They all go through the motions of living, "nobody's authentic" (*ER* 69). The person behind the gestures doesn't exist.

Three "doctrines" are offered in the course of the novel as ways out of the void. One could call them the prescriptive, the subjectivist, and the objectivist doctrines.

The first is offered as early as chapter 1—a splendid chapter, into which many of the novel's central issues are effortlessly condensed. It is a doctrine offered, appropriately, by a doctor at the "Remobilization Farm." "You will teach prescriptive grammar," he tells Jake. "No description at all. No optimal situations. Teach the rules. Teach the truth about grammar."

The "truth about grammar" is the truth of logic, of an aprioristic system of rules. It gives up all correspondence with reality ("no description at all") and thrives on its own inner coherence. As such, it is a caricature of solipsistic rationalism, a heightened analogue of the rationalism of Kafka's heroes, who insist on understanding the "inexplicable mass of rock." "Were there some arguments in his favor that had been overlooked?" asks Joseph K. in *The Trial*, while the hands of the executioners are already at his throat. Never overlook any argument in your favor, regardless of the hands of the executioners at your throat: this is the prescriptive doctrine.

Diametrically opposed, it seems, is the way of Jake's colleague Joe, the way I called subjectivist. Joe, the "history man," would be "a fish out of water in the prescriptive racket," for Joe believes that "paths shall be laid where people walk, instead of walking where the paths happen to be laid" (*ER* 22). He believes in less-than-absolutes (*ER* 43), in psychological givens (*ER* 46). He isn't impressed by unity, harmony, eternality, and universality (ibid.). "The most a man can ever do," he says, "is be right from his point of view."

This *seems* the opposite of the prescriptive—but it isn't. For it soon turns out that Joe's subjectivism is self-prescriptive, that he is a slave to the silly aim of "living coherently" (*ER* 55). His insistence on following the psychological givens—as in sending his wife Rennie to sleep again with Jake because she once showed she wanted it—is an insane reasonableness (*ER* 143), no less cerebral and alienated from reality than prescriptivism. This, I suppose, is what Rennie intuits when she tells Jake that "in a lot of ways you're *not* totally different from Joe. . . . You work from a lot of the same premises" (*ER* 63).

It is in connection with the third, "objectivist" doctrine that Wittgenstein's words are quoted (*ER* 80). Once again it is the doctor who is responsible for this doctrine. He is now described by Jake as "Father Divine," "some combination of quack and prophet" (*ER* 84). Indeed, his conversation with Jake has some affinities with the priest's exchange with Joseph K. in that it ends with a similar rejection of truth: " 'All right, then,' I said at last, giving up. 'Everything you say is true. All of it is the truth.' The Doctor listened calmly. 'You don't know what you're talking about,' he said. 'There's no such thing as truth as you conceive it' " (*ER* 82). Compare *The Trial:* " 'I don't agree with that point of view,' said K. shaking his head, 'for if one accepts it, one must accept as true everything the door-keeper says. But you yourself have sufficiently proved how impossible it is to do that.' 'No,' said the priest, 'it is not necessary to accept everything as true, one must only accept it as necessary' " (*T* 243). The necessity of facts, rather than their truth, is also the Doctor's message. His present version of necessity has nothing to do with logical necessity, with his original "truth about grammar." Logic, it now transpires, has nothing to teach. There is no logical reason why the Cleveland Municipal Stadium should seat exactly 707,700, "but it happens that it does": "There's no reason in the long run why Italy shouldn't be shaped like a sausage instead of a boot, but that doesn't happen to be the case. *The world is everything that is the case*, and what the case is is not a matter of logic" (*ER* 80). One must therefore give up reason—give up "prescriptive grammar"—and turn to "informational therapy." Instead of "no description at all," description becomes all. What counts now is random, inexplicable chance, whatever happens to be "the case."

The divorce between reason and reality, which in the first two doctrines led to a rejection of reality, now leads to a rejection of reason. This is the Kafkaesque doctrine that is no doctrine at all, because what it amounts to is that the world is what it is, that "the incomprehensible is incomprehensible" (*CS* 457). Jake must bow to the tyranny of arbitrary fact—to the 707,700 seats—just as Joseph K. must bow to the tyranny of the doorkeeper, because the doorkeeper "belongs to the Law and as such is set beyond human judgement."

The blank center about which Jake moves, blindly gesticulating, constantly switching from one role to another, makes his life story as tentative as any "legend" in Kafka. In the same way that each of the four legends concerning Prometheus is a desperate attempt to give pattern to the inexplicable mass of rock, Jake's story is one single attempt to fill the gap at the center of his being. He is perfectly aware of the bearings his situation has on its telling: if "in a sense" he is Jake Horner (*ER* 5), his story is "in a sense" the story of his life, for "the same life lends itself to any number of stories" (*ER* 8). The essences he assigns to people are analogous to the essences a tale-teller must reduce his characters to, ignoring their "charming complexities" if he is "to get on with the plot" (*ER* 29). This metafictional element became central in the later Barth.[4]

If *The End of the Road*, in spite of its many affinities with Kafka, is less than a Kafkaesque novel, this is precisely because the gap is at the center of *Jake's* being, not of being as such. In other words, it is because the novel is basically psychological, not metaphysical. Or rather, its metaphysical findings are subordinated to a particular psychological makeup, Jake Horner's. Horner, unlike K., is too individualized, too contrasted to other human types to be Everyman. His eyes are sightless not because of the innate inadequacy of the human mind, but because he is an emotional cripple. The void, thus, is his, not the world's. Gestic theater, inauthenticity, severance from doctrine, tentative interpretations with nothing to interpret—all the components of Kafka's world are internalized, individualized, and thus relativized.

To put it in more theoretical terms, the gap at the level of the *sjužet* (How is Jake to get out of the void of unlimited choice?) is filled in unsuccessfully (the three doctrines) and becomes permanent. But it is a gap to Jake, not to the reader; it is psychologically motivated and therefore not absolute. As such, it is acceptable to the reader and does not call for symbolic reading. The story is metonymically relatable to the world at large, an instance of the psychology of a certain human type. It is therefore conventional in the final analysis, lacking the specifically Kafkaesque gap at the thematic level. Barth does not condemn himself to shouting a meaningless message because his concern is not with the world as a totality; his concern is with the particular despair of a particular man who thought he could see the world as a totality.

II　One cannot think of a novel more different from *The End of the Road* than Vonnegut's *Cat's Cradle*. If the former is realistic, clean-cut, crystalline, and well-knit, the latter is fantastic, arbitrary, and jumpy. The anti-utopian island of San Lorenzo, with its conflicting religions, its instrument of punishment (the "hook"), and the outsider-narrator called to become its new president, bears what seems a more than accidental resemblance to Kafka's "In the Penal Colony."[5] More important, however, is its deeper Kafkaesque level: the self-canceling message at its center.

In a sense, this deeper level too can be related to "In the Penal Colony." For if the murderous machine in Kafka's story must kill the officer, its most fanatic adherent, in order to assert itself against the new liberalism,[6] Vonnegut's "hook" asserts the "Bokononist" religion by executing its own devotees.[7] But Vonnegut outdoes Kafka (and also falls short of him, I shall argue) by making self-cancelation an integral, thematic ingredient of the very "religion" he devises. This paradoxical strategy precedes the narrative itself: the first epigraph, "Nothing in this book is true," is the logical conundrum known as the Paradox of the Liar. If it is true, it is false;

if false, true. If the narrator is telling the truth in saying that nothing in this book is true, these words also aren't true. Thus, he is both telling the truth and lying. Incidentally, he is also canceling his second epigraph, a quotation from "The Books of Bokonon": "Live by the *foma* [harmless untruths] that makes you brave and kind and healthy and happy." If nothing in this book is true, this commendation of untruth is also untrue.

Thus, the entire novel is presented a priori as one big violation of a basic law of logic, the law of contradiction: its statements are both true and false. This, of course, could be said of any work of fiction: that it is neither true nor false, or, for that matter, both true and false. But the same logically impossible status is conferred on Bokononism itself, the "doctrine" at the center of the novel. In other words, not only plot and characters but the novel's very "thesis" (in Beardsley's sense) is fictitious, both claiming and disclaiming itself. Thus, for instance, Bokonon presents an elaborate cosmogony only to dismiss it as a pack of lies (*CC* 129–30). Moreover, on the title page of his "First Book" he warns the reader: "Don't be a fool! Close this book at once! It is nothing but *foma!*" (*CC* 177).

He does exactly what Vonnegut does on the back of his own title page. Both the novel and its "doctrine" lie when they tell the truth and tell the truth when they lie. Should one listen to Bokonon and close his book at once? Yes, because the book declares that it is nothing but *foma;* i.e., it declares that what it declares is *foma;* i.e., that the book is anything but *foma;* i.e., that one should *not* close the book. This is the "cruel paradox of Bokononist thought, the heartbreaking necessity of lying about reality, and the heartbreaking impossibility of lying about it" (*CC* 189). But this, too, is *foma*, I suppose.

A parallel logical difficulty is the yoking together of Providence and chance in Bokononist lore. This appears as early as the first paragraph of the novel, where the Melvillian opening ("Call me Jonah") is explained: "Jonah . . . because somebody or something has compelled me to be certain places at certain times, without fail . . . according to plan, at each appointed second, at each appointed place this Jonah was there" (*CC* 11). "Compelled," "appointed," "without fail," "according to plan" strongly imply Providence. But all that Providence amounts to is being "certain places at certain times." One cannot help being certain places at certain times, of course, but why call it plan? An unknown plan is no plan; a "somebody or something" is no God. If humanity, according to Bokonon, is organized into teams that "do God's will without ever discovering what they are doing" (*CC* 11), God's will becomes "everything that is the case." Salvation, as in Kafka, becomes the randomly given present moment, is everywhere, is nowhere. "As it was *supposed* to happen"—the Bokononist version of "as it happened"—is a senseless insistence that what is meaningless has meaning, what is patternless has pattern. The formulas of Providence are filled with the empty pronouns of the void: "by that time Johnson [i.e., Bokonon] had developed a conviction that *something* was trying to get him *somewhere* for *some* reason" (*CC* 76; my italics). Bokonon is obviously a king's courier, not a king; he is posting through the world shouting formulas of faith emptied of faith.

This emptiness, as in Kafka, often bears the form of tautology. "Each of us has to be what he or she is"; "animals breathe in what animals breathe out, and vice versa" (*CC* 178–79): these are some of the "secrets of life" Bokonon teaches and the narrator follows. Meaninglessness also bears the form of a mirror image, as in the Bürgel episode: the stone angel that a German immigrant orders as a tombstone for his wife but never comes to claim has, the narrator feels, "puzzling spiritual implications" (*CC* 58). But what are they? The name inscribed on its pedestal, first concealed by the boughs banked against it, later turns out to be the narrator's own name (*CC* 56). The angel's message is a mirror image of its receiver.

The central "picture of the meaninglessness of it all" (*CC* 116), a *mise-en-abyme* of the entire novel, is the cat's cradle itself. Painted by Newt Hoenikker, it consists of spider's-web-like scratches in black impasto, meaning both everything and nothing. On one hand, "it means something different to everyone who sees it" (*CC* 113); on the other hand, it is "nothing but a bunch of *x*'s between somebody's hands. . . . No damn cat, and no damn cradle" (*CC*

114). Finally, its meaning is reduced to self-mirroring tautology, to a truth about grammar: "It means whatever it means" (*CC* 115). When another character, Julian Castle, responds to this tautology with "Then it's hell," he is as wrong as Joseph K. is when he responds to the priest's dictum that "it is not necessary to accept everything as true, one must only accept it as necessary," with the words: "A melancholy conclusion. It turns lying into a universal principle." Truth is deposed by the priest to be replaced not by lying, as K. thinks, but by necessity. K.'s words, "Lying [is] a universal principle" are a statement about the world as a totality and therefore as impossible as "truth is a universal principle." Instead, one must abandon the categories of rational judgment altogether and opt for mere acceptance. "It means whatever it means" rather than hell (or paradise, for that matter) is Vonnegut's final position, too. His narrator's dream has been to climb San Lorenzo's highest mountain "with some magnificent symbol" and plant it there. What he finds at the end is that his hands are utterly empty of symbols (*CC* 190).

The disappearance of the symbol is tantamount to the loss of doctrine in Kafka. For the symbol, as Paul de Man puts it, "is founded on an intimate unity between the image that rises up before the senses and the supersensory totality that the image suggests."[8] In Kafka the image—the *Aggadah*—rises up before the senses, but it has lost its intimate unity with the supersensory totality, with the *Halakhah,* which is no longer recoverable. Vonnegut, however, though his narrator's hands are empty of symbols, does not relinquish the supersensory meaning of his images. This meaning, on the contrary, is perfectly recoverable from his fictive world; indeed, it is explicitly given in Bokonon's lore. The paradoxical coexistence of truth and lying, of pattern and chance, is here thematized, becomes a comment of the world at large, not a means of making such a comment impossible. The end of "The Books of Bokonon," the end of the novel, and the end of the world overlap, all joining to corroborate Bokonon's final gesture of "thumbing his nose at You Know Who"—a blatantly unambiguous gesture, not at all "a subject for reflection without end."

III   Pynchon's *V.* too, though for different reasons, lacks the status of Kafka's fiction. Each of its many plots and episodes may show the open-ended structure that is typical of Kafka, but the very repetition of the same structure makes necessary the thematic extrapolation that Kafka avoids.

If Kafka finds himself at the bottom of a ravine unable to take a broad view of matters, Stencil, the key figure of *V.,* is situated at the bottom of a fold in the wrinkled surface of twentieth-century history, unable "to determine warp, woof or pattern anywhere else" (*V.* 141). He is therefore "lost to any sense of a continuous tradition" (ibid.). His quest for the broad view, for continuity, unity, doctrine, is his quest for the mysterious lady "V." V. is Pynchon's *Halakhah.*

V. is "a remarkably scattered concept"; "disguise is one of her attributes" (*V.* 364, 363): these are two of the ironically understated references to the endless impersonations—man, woman, town, anything—with which V. confronts Stencil. The novel dissolves into many episodes, each groping toward the ever-elusive doctrine, each using a different historical setting and a different literary style in an attempt to get at it.[9] These are so many scenes in a gestic theater, wild postures vis-à-vis a "universe of things which simply are" (*V.* 307), vis-à-vis the inexplicable mass of rock, which here becomes rocky Malta and its seaport Valletta, perhaps the most basic version of V.

Kafka's "Prometheus" can shed light on the stunning proliferation of plots in *V.* In "Prometheus," the reader may recall, four different legends concerning Prometheus are all dismissed as ephemeral attempts at explaining the "inexplicable mass of rock" that alone remains. The number four is accidental, of course; there is no limit to the number of legends, once their necessary inadequacy is conceded. This seems to be the principle governing Pynchon's novel.

Its numberless plots, characters, narrative levels, and styles are all, to use the beautiful image with which the novel ends, surface phenomena on the Mediterranean, "whitecaps, kelp islands, any of a million flatnesses which should catch thereafter part of the brute sun's spectrum," and they show nothing at all of what lies beneath

(*V.* 463). And yet, the riddle of existence and Stencil's quest for it lend these surface phenomena a surprisingly rigid unity. "The stone's in the midst of all," as Yeats puts it.

The stoniness, or rockiness, of the riddle in the midst of all is one unifying element. Not only is the rocky town of Valletta one of V.'s disguises, but a "progression toward inanimateness" (*V.* 385) is a feature common to all her impersonations. She has "an obsession with bodily incorporating little bits of inert matter" (*V.* 459), and inert matter, *hyle,* is the translogical, the incomprehensible (*V.* 455). The boy with the golden screw for a navel (*V.* 30), or the disintegrating "Bad Priest," who gradually sheds false hair, false teeth, false eyes, and false feet (*V.* 321–22) are two examples of the inanimateness that pervades V.'s metamorphoses and symbolizes her imperviousness to reason.

Another unifying element is the way reason copes, or rather doesn't cope, with what is impervious to it. In many of the episodes the quest leads to a pseudorevelation that is basically Kafkaesque. It is often either banal or tautological, or, most important, mirrorlike, reminiscent, however remotely, of the Bürgel episode. Its recurrence gives this wildly sprawling novel the unity of a series of variations on an obsessive theme.

Take the boy with the golden screw for a navel. He appears very early in the novel, in a dream dreamt by Profane, the other key figure in the novel besides Stencil. After twenty years of consulting specialists all over the world on how to get rid of the screw, he gets to a voodoo doctor in Haiti. All trappings of imminent revelation follow, complete with potion, sleep, and red balloon, until the secret cure is revealed: a screwdriver—and not just a screwdriver, but one "with a yellow plastic handle," the commonest of them all (*V.* 30).

Or take the disintegration of the Bad Priest, one of the most forceful episodes in the novel. To the children's mocking question, "What is your sermon for today?" the priest responds with a gradual coming apart—priest into woman (with a star sapphire in her navel this time) into a horribly mutilated trunk. Having no oil with which to anoint the dying "woman" and perform the sacrament of extreme unction, the narrator (now the Maltese poet Fausto Maijstral) uses instead her own blood, "dipping it from the navel as from a chalice" (*V.* 323). Thus, the priest's final "sermon," his message, is a gradual shedding of all appearances in order to get to the core. But the core, imagined rather than revealed, is all fragile make-believe ("intestines of parti-colored silk, gay balloon-lungs, a rococo heart"), and the final redemptive sacrament is tautological: the bleeding woman is anointed with her own blood. No deity is there for the dying to unite with and be blessed. There is no message from beyond. The very blood is a mockery of the final message, a mirror image of the bleeding self.

To go on and show all the other variations on this theme would require a discussion of many of the novel's images: Vheissu, the remote mysterious place and the "Nothing" lurking beneath its "skin" (*V.* 188); the South Pole, where Godolphin sees the "light," which turns out to be the corpse of a spider monkey (*V.* 189); the Venus of Botticelli's "Birth of Venus," both uncovered and covered (*V.* 162); "Shroud," the plastic mannikin for radiation tests with nothing under its shell (*V.* 346–47); V. in love with the dancer Melanie, watching her watching herself in the mirror, her mirror image contemplating V. (*V.* 385). The same basic structure—quest ending in a travesty of revelation—repeats everywhere. But let me dwell on one outstanding case.

I am referring to Mondaugen's story (chapter 9). The story of the young engineering student, sent to a white outpost in South-West Africa to study the mysterious "sferic" signals, abounds with Kafkaesque allusions: Kurt (K.!) Mondaugen, the engineer, is the counterpart of K. the land surveyor; the natives are poised against Foppl's fortress like the villagers versus the Castle; the fortress, a place of mirrors with the sun reflected in its windows, giving it a supernatural aura, is reminiscent of the Castle as it appears to K. in the first chapter of *The Castle;* the whipped native combines the whipping scene from *The Trial* with the punishment apparatus from "In the Penal Colony"; the General who is to come back and punish them all, "like Jesus returning to earth" (*V.* 222), is like the Commandant in "In the Penal Colony"; Foppl, "the agent of [the General's] will," "sick of more than simple enthusiasm," "under compulsion" to recreate the past (*V.* 222–23), is clearly modeled on the officer in the same story, and so on.

Most important, however, are the "sferics" and their final decoding. They include whistles, clicks, and also something "like a warbling of birds called the dawn chorus" (*V.* 213), very much like the spheric music, "the echo of voices singing at an infinite distance," that K. hears over the phone, a mysterious message from the Castle (*C* 33). When it is finally decoded by a character called Weissman (the knower? he is a companion of Vera, the True One), the message turns out to be: "Kurt Mondaugen, Die Welt ist alles was der Fall ist" (*V.* 258).

Mondaugen translates, "The world is all that the case is," and adds: "I've heard that somewhere before." The irony is twofold: he has heard that somewhere before not only because Heaven is quoting Wittgenstein (and Barth!), but because the ultimate secret turns out to be a blatant tautology: the world is what it is, and, to quote Kafka's "On Parables," "we know that already" (*CS* 457). Similarly unhelpful is the first part of the message, "Kurt Mondaugen," a mere mirror image of the quester. "What a joke," it is said about Stencil elsewhere in the novel, "if at the end of this hunt he came face to face with himself afflicted by a kind of soul-transvestism" (*V.* 210).

It is a measure of the obsessiveness of this theme in Pynchon that the heroine of his next book, *The Crying of Lot 49* (1965), makes a similar discovery. Oedipa Mass's quest for the secret of "the Tristero," her dead lover's legacy, ends with the suspicion that the "legacy was America," that "she might have found The Tristero anywhere in her Republic, through any of a hundred lightly-concealed entranceways, a hundred alienations, if only she'd looked."[10] The Tristero, in other words, is "all that the case is." *The Crying of Lot 49* could very well serve as another episode in *V.*

In a sense Pynchon may be said to out-Kafka Kafka in the emphasis he puts on the tentativeness of the single "legend," and the ensuing multiplication of legends in *V.* The gap at the center of being leads to a compulsive heaping of plot on plot, episode on episode, all equally tentative, equally replaceable. Paradoxically, however, the uniform structure of these episodes—quest for secret meaning ending in banal, tautological, or self-mirroring "revelation"—must reduce the openness of Kafka's single-plot stories to a single theme: the futility of all our attempts to understand the world we live in. The episodes are repetitive rather than tentative, and through sheer repetition, sheer insistence on a similarly structured vehicle, the vehicle is foregrounded and becomes the tenor itself. Quest and failure, in Kafka, are there only to point to their unspecified object, a subject for reflection without end. Here, quest and failure are the subject itself.

IV   The difference between Kafka's achievement and that of his American followers—as well as his other followers discussed in this book—can be described in terms of the difference between two versions of Jesus' answer when asked about parables. According to Mark, he tells his disciples: "Unto you it is given to know the mystery of the kingdom of God: But unto them that are without, all these things are done in parables: That seeing they may see, and not perceive; and hearing they may hear, and not understand; lest at any time they should be converted, and their sins should be forgiven them" (Mark 4:11–12). Matthew's version is different: "Therefore speak I to them in parables: because they seeing see not; and hearing they hear not, neither do they understand." The difference between the two versions hinges on "that" ("that . . . they may see and not perceive") versus "because" ("because they . . . see not"); that is, parables are designed to mystify according to Mark, to clarify according to Matthew. Frank Kermode, in *The Genesis of Secrecy,* calls the first the "*hina* doctrine" (*hina* is the Greek for "that"), and the second the "*hoti* doctrine" (*hoti* means "because"). According to the first, narrative is intentionally esoteric; according to the second it clarifies. Kafka, says Kermode, belongs to the first: "Kafka, like Mark . . . supports what might be called the *hina* doctrine of narrative. The desire to change *hina* to *hoti* is a measure of the dismay we feel at our arbitrary and total exclusion from the kingdom, or from the secret sense of the story, of which we learn—by its radiance—only that it is overwhelmingly important."[11] These American authors, I may add, belong rather to the *hoti* doctrine of narrative. No matter how pessimistic their novels, they do not finally banish us from the secret places of their narratives. In this sense they narrate to clarify. Kafka does not.

In the first chapter I said that the way post-Kafkan writers misread Kafka explains much of their achievement. I would add now that it sheds no less light on his own. There is no better way of reaching a clear concept of Kafka's own unique strength than through examining the works of his followers. What they borrowed from him must bring to mind what they failed to borrow. Considering what they failed to borrow must lead to the question of how what they did borrow relates to what they did not borrow. And the coexistence of the two in Kafka himself must lead to a clearer definition of his unique achievement.

Take Sartre. What he had the insight to borrow from Kafka, in *Nausea,* was the incomprehensible metamorphosis of man into brute matter; what he seems to have missed was the literalness of that occurrence. Instead, he psychologized it and rewrote it as his protagonist's daydreaming, revising Kafka's (partial) *merveilleux* into *l'étrange.* By thus saving psychological realism, he taught us where Kafka's strength lies: precisely in the irreducible presentation of the incomprehensible.

Camus, in *The Outsider,* opted for psychological realism in a different way. He borrowed Joseph K.'s ignorance of his inner life, but limited it to the particular psychomoral makeup of his own protagonist Meursault. It was now an individual rebel's alienation from collective standards of feeling, not Everyman's incomprehension of himself. Camus thus taught us that Kafka's silence concerning human motivation is not a rejection of the moral values of a particular culture, but total epistemological agnosticism. This agnosticism makes Kafka relinquish not only the privileges of the omniscient narrator, but also those of the single-consciousness story: his single consciousness is blind to much of its own content.

Kafka's agnosticism, which emerges from an examination of his misinterpretation by Sartre and Camus, is likewise implicit in the way his American followers—Barth, Vonnegut, and Pynchon—have revised him. What they have taken from Kafka is the plot pattern of quest ending in pseudorevelation; what they resisted was Kafka's refusal to let this plot be translated into the terms of any of the systems that we use to understand our reality. They resisted, in other words, his rejection of theme. Unlike Kafka, they tell a referential story that comments on the real world. Thus, they remind us that Kafka tells a story that does not.

Robbe-Grillet and Beckett teach us the same lesson, but obversely. If the Americans, like Kafka, have a story but, unlike Kafka, also have a theme, Robbe-Grillet and Beckett, like Kafka, do not have a theme but, unlike Kafka, do not have a story either. Kafka's skepticism, which forbids the reduction of his stories to definite themes, here extends to the story itself, shattering it into a hundred fragments. This collapse of narrative along with truth, of *Aggadah* along with *Halakhah,* sets off the uniqueness of Kafka's achievement in clinging to *Aggadah* while eschewing *Halakhah,* or sacrificing truth, to quote Benjamin again, for the sake of clinging to its transmissibility.

Beckett, in *Watt,* Robbe-Grillet, and Agnon, repeat Kafkaesque motifs but do not follow Kafka's use of language. If Kafka's language largely withdraws to the background, relinquishing all pretense to salvation, their language—or, in the case of Robbe-Grillet, narrative technique—is drastically foregrounded, becomes "semantic succour." Thus, they remind us, each in his very different way, that Kafka's blatant presentation of the incomprehensible is never sidetracked by the comforts of language.

Is it never sidetracked by art itself? On the contrary.

Perhaps the most astounding paradox about Kafka is that the writer who is popularly the most "relevant" of them all, the writer who "invented" bureaucracy and concentration camps, seems also to be the most resolute champion of a modernistic version of *art pour l'art.* For isn't this heroic making of myths without theme the desperate creation of fictions for their own sake? These stories, by defeating all attempts to translate them into truth, must always send readers back to themselves. Their refusal to yield an unambiguous message seems to be a celebration of pure fictionality, of pure art.

In this, Kafka's stories are part and parcel of modernity. They resemble an extreme expression of what is perhaps the *differentia specifica* of modernism: its disinterestedness, its renunciation of both mimesis and self-expression, its insistence on the autonomy of art, and its independence from empirical experience. Kafka's "sacrifice of truth" could thus serve as a perfect motto for modernism. But could it? Surely what seems to common sensibility so "relevant" in Kafka cannot be simply dismissed. Surely the theological interpretation of a Max Brod—let alone that of a Gershom Scholem— must have some anchor in Kafka's work. Paradoxically, the very irreducibility of his work to a truth is a measure of its obsession with the truth. As suggested earlier, I believe that Kafka's self-reflexiveness is inseparable from the metaphysical thrust of his work. Unwilling to accept any understanding that is not ultimate and total, he keeps sending his allegorizers back to the hard facts of his parables.

This is the uniquely paradoxical status of Kafka's fiction. It constantly displays its metaphorical face, its lack of self-sufficiency, its reaching to a truth beyond itself; but it constantly evades that truth, pointing stubbornly back to itself. This never-ending oscillation between parable and reality is what the little dialogue at the end of Kafka's "On Parables" enacts:

> Concerning this [the gap between parables and daily cares] a man once said: Why such reluctance? If you only followed the parables you yourselves would become parables and with that rid of all your daily cares.
>
> Another said: I bet that is also a parable.
>
> The first said: You have won.
>
> The second said: But unfortunately only in parable.
>
> The first said: No, in reality: in parable you have lost.
>
> (CS 457)

That night Mr. Heilprin and I happened to visit a cafe where we used to go on days devoid of pleasure. Mr. Heilprin is highborn of an ancient family, one of those distinguished families of Israel that have sustained us during our long exile and given us power to stand among the nations. Sometimes, be he in high spirits or low, when surrounded by willing listeners, he recounts the glory of his ancestors. Having studied secular sciences rather than the Torah, he does not boast of his ancestors' learning. Instead, he describes their homes and business dealings. And even from these everyday matters one hears how gracious were those early generations and how gracious their deeds. And one's soul weeps in secret for the pride of Israel, wrested from them and not to return till the coming of the Messiah.

Mr. Heilprin was still talking when the clock struck. He flicked the ash from his cigarette, looked at me sorrowfully and asked, "How will you get home? I think that the bus to your neighborhood stops running after ten o'clock in the evening." I looked at my watch and said, "If I hurry, I'll catch it on my way." I made my departure and left. My throat being sore, I wrapped a scarf around my neck against the chill. I turned off into a quiet side street where there were no passers-by. People in a hurry had better choose a way not made for crowds, as broad streets are full of obstacles. Not only people, but even those vehicles intended for our use obstruct us pedestrians.

The side street into which I turned was shaped like the Hebrew letter lamed, with two rows of stone houses inhabited by working folk. Such people go to bed at dusk and rise to go to work

From S. Y. Agnon, *Samukh Venir'e* (Jerusalem and Tel-Aviv: Schocken, 1950), pp. 191–95. © World copyright Schocken Publishing House, Tel-Aviv, Israel. This translation by Tirza Sandbank.

at dawn, and from dusk to dawn the streets are empty and one can walk to one's heart's content with no worry of being waylaid by passers-by.

Thus I walked between the two rows of houses, which were sleeping the sleep of laborers, like those who have only the few hours of a short night to rest their weary bones. The houses already slumbered and were draped in heavy shadows that sprawled in front of me like a wall. The further I went the denser the shadows became and the darkness closed in. I knew they were only shadows, but they seemed like a wall. I began to fear that the road would end in a cul-de-sac and that I would be forced to go all the way back and thus miss the bus. When one is in a hurry and there is only one bus, every shadow becomes a wall.

To return or not to return? If I returned, I might find the bus gone. If I did not, I would have to return later on, for the way might really turn out to be closed. In any case, there was no point in lingering there. Or perhaps I should go to the end of the road and find out whether there was some opening in the wall, and if there was, I should examine where it led to.

I heard a noise behind me like the fall of footsteps, and I realized that somebody was following me. I did not turn my head to see who it was. Who could it be? The father of a sick child looking for a doctor or a pharmacy? A workman who had wasted his last penny in a bar? In any case, I could not sustain him in his need. These were hard times. Many in need of help and little to be done.

Suddenly, a heavy hand grasped the scarf on my neck. What could it be? If somebody was trying to tell me something, did he have to grasp my scarf just now when my throat hurt? If my scarf fell off, my cold might get worse. Perhaps he wanted nothing from me, but was just playing a joke. If a joke, not a very good one.

Wisely enough, I did not rebuke him. If I had, he would have replied, we would have quarreled, and I would have been delayed. After all, I was in a hurry to get home and go to bed. Sitting in coffeehouses first seems pleasurable enough, but in the end one's body aches, nor is one's soul spared.

So I did not scold that jester but, on the contrary, smiled at him, as if I liked his silly joke. I thought to myself that since he was rewarded amply by my acknowledgment of his joke, he would leave me alone and go away.

He, however, had other plans. I smiled at him and he smiled back, but from his smile I could see that something was amiss. There was a fiendish look in his eyes. I pretended not to notice and said to him, "I have a cold, and I wrapped this woolen scarf around my neck because a woolen scarf is good for a sore throat."

The man looked first to one side, then to the other, as if he had secretly summoned witnesses and was now beckoning to them to come out. What had I done wrong to make him hold onto my scarf and not let go? What crime had I committed to make him bring witnesses against me? I wanted to leave my scarf in his hands and go my way. Then I changed my mind: if I left him my scarf, he would have reason to suspect me. I stood still. Many thoughts went through my mind. I was sure the man had mistaken me for somebody else. But for whom, I wondered. I should have asked him, but I had not. I had a cold, and my throat was sore, and I knew that my voice trembled. A trembling voice at night, in a narrow alley far from town, might cause suspicion.

He scolded me and said, "Come along." Let's go along without arguing, I said to myself. After all, wherever he brings me, they will see that I am innocent and release me. I walked after him, my head bent.

We walked for a while, and I found myself in a large room. A smell of sleepers pervaded the room. A heavy darkness seemed to oppress my whole body. Even my hair, which was standing on end, seemed to droop.

Suddenly a little lamp was lit, one of those little lamps that presume surprisingly to do away with darkness. In front of me I saw a man neither young nor old, reclining on a high bed full of pillows and quilts. He had a thick handlebar mustache, its turned-up ends white and its middle black. He seemed confused, as someone who had just woken from sleep. I thought that he would be angry at having been woken up, and that, being angry at whoever awakened him, he would also be angry at me, who was the cause of it all. I made myself as small as possible, so that he should not notice me, and I looked at the lamp, whose light seemed to bite into the room like an insect biting another insect.

He lifted his head from the pillows and stood up, putting on a many-cornered hat like the hats that present-day cantors wear, considered elegant but in fact ugly. This, however, was no cantor's hat, but a hat of the secret police. He put it straight and said something. I did not hear what he said, but was surprised to notice that he did not speak harshly.

My companion said something in reply. I did not hear what he said, but was surprised to notice that he spoke to him as to a brother. All that while I stood at some distance from the secretary. Since I saw he was treating me fairly, I wanted to tell him who I was, in the hope that he would lighten my sentence. In the end I decided to remain silent, with the expectation that he would not pass judgment before questioning me.

He asked me nothing, but sat down at his desk, took up pen, paper, and ink, and started writing. The room was silent and the smell of kerosene wafted from the lamp. There was no sound save the scratching of the pen on the paper. As long as the pen did not break and the paper did not tear, he would not stop his writing. I stood still in the same place pondering whether the middle part of his mustache had not grown white. It had not, but its two ends seemed darker.

At long last he finished writing, sprinkled some sand on the paper and looked toward me courteously. I looked at him questioningly, as if to ask leave to go. His face was sealed. It was impossible to detect either a yes or a no. O that imponderable face, revealing nothing, its stare riveting me to my place. Thus, I stood immobile. This state was not an unpleasurable one, in that it was like all those states that exempt us from action.

As long as the pen wrote, its sound was heard. Now that it was silent, I could hear the strains of Jewish voices coming from the corridor, and I knew that while I had been standing there waiting for my verdict, other Jews had been brought in.

The door opened and I could see an old man seated, his quavering voice chanting a prayer, while some of his brethren assisted him. How had this weak old man come here? Just yesterday he had been prostrate on his sickbed. And what was he doing in this house chanting prayers? Catching sight of me, he raised his voice, uttering a few obscenities in the same melody, the melody of prayer. I rebuked him and said, "Have you gone mad?" He smiled to himself and responded, still in melody, "I do not belong to the authorities and neither do you, my friend, so what do you care?" All his friends, all those Jews who were with him, nodded and said, "True, very true," and then went back to their singing, a song mingling prayer with obscenity.

Notes

1 Truth and Transmissibility

1   Walter Benjamin, *Illuminations,* ed. Hannah Arendt, trans. Harry Zohn (New York: Harcourt, Brace and World, 1968), pp. 147, 120, 122. In the epigraph to this chapter and elsewhere I use "aggadic" and "Aggadah," rather than "haggadic" and "Haggadah," as wrongly spelled by Benjamin and his English translator. Gershom Scholem, in his German translation of the Hebrew poet Ch. N. Bialik's essay "Halakhah and Aggadah" (Ch. N. Bialik, "Halacha und Aggada," trans. G. Scholem, *Der Jude* 4 [1919–20]: 61–77), an essay that doubtless inspired Benjamin's use of the terms, spells "Aggada" with an *A*.

2   *Encyclopaedia Judaica* (Jerusalem: Keter, 1971), 2:vii.

3   Ibid., pp. 354–55.

4   Benjamin, *Illuminations,* p. 122.

5   I use "theme" in Monroe C. Beardsley's sense of what is relatable to the real world, as distinct from "subject," which refers to the fictive world. See his *Aesthetics* (New York: Harcourt, Brace and World, 1958), p. 403.

6   I owe the terms and concepts used here to Shlomith Rimmon, *The Concept of Ambiguity—The Example of James* (Chicago: University of Chicago Press, 1977). Some of Rimmon's fine distinctions, not needed for my present discussion, are ignored.

7   From Roland Barthes, *S/Z,* as quoted in English translation in Jonathan Culler, *Structuralist Poetics* (Ithaca, N.Y.: Cornell University Press, Cornell Paperback, 1977), p. 227.

8   Culler, *Structuralist Poetics,* p. 230.

9   "Wie sie sich geben mögen, ehe sie sich mir zeigen"—"Gespräch mit dem Beter," in F. Kafka, *Erzählungen und kleine Prosa* (New York: Schocken, 1946), p. 17.

10 Throughout this book the following initials are used for Kafka's works:

    CS *The Complete Stories,* ed. Nahum N. Glatzer (New York: Schocken, 1976).

    T   *The Trial,* trans. Willa Muir and Edwin Muir (Harmondsworth: Penguin, 1972).

    C   *The Castle,* trans. Willa Muir and Edwin Muir, with additional material translated by Eithne Wilkins and Ernst Kaiser (Harmondsworth: Penguin, 1963).

D   *The Diaries of Franz Kafka 1910–23,* ed. Max Brod, trans. Joseph Kresh and Martin Greenberg, with the cooperation of Hannah Arendt (Harmondsworth: Penguin, 1964).

11 "Despair" (Verzweiflung) in the original, rather than "bewilderment," as in the English translation.

12 Jacques Derrida, "Devant la Loi," in *Philosophy and Literature,* ed. A. Phillips Griffiths, Royal Institute of Philosophy Lecture Series, no. 16 (Cambridge: Cambridge University Press, 1984), pp. 173–88.

13 Jonathan Culler, *On Deconstruction. Theory and Criticism after Structuralism* (London: Routledge and Kegan Paul, 1983), p. 86.

14 For a detailed analysis, see Shimon Sandbank, "Structures of Paradox in Kafka," *Modern Language Quarterly* 28 (1967): 469–71.

15 *The Great Wall of China. Stories and Reflections,* trans. Willa Muir and Edwin Muir (New York: Schocken, 1946), p. 289.

16 Harold Bloom, *The Anxiety of Influence* (New York: Oxford University Press, 1973), p. 30.

2 *Kafka's Insect and Sartre's Crab*

1 J.-P. Sartre, *What Is Literature?,* trans. B. Frechtman (London: Methuen, 1950), p. 168.

2 For Kafka's reception in France, see Marthe Robert's chapter in Hartmut Binder, ed., *Kafka-Handbuch* (Stuttgart: Alfred Kroener, 1979), 2:681–87. Cf. Peter U. Beicken, *Franz Kafka: Eine kritische Einführung in die Forschung* (Frankfurt am Main: Athenäum Fischer, 1974), pp. 42–43. Beicken largely follows an earlier contribution by Robert, "Kafka en France," *Mercure de France* (June 1961): 241–55.

3 "'Aminadab' ou du fantastique considéré comme un langage," *Cahiers du Sud* (April–May 1943); reprinted in *Situations I* (Paris: Gallimard, 1947). Here quoted from Annette Michelson's English version in Sartre, *Literary and Philosophical Essays* (New York: Collier, 1962), pp. 60–77. Hereinafter cited *LPE.*

4 Cf. Selma Fraiberg, "Kafka and the Dream," *Partisan Review* 23, no. 1 (1956): 47–69. This "lack of astonishment" on the part of Kafka's heroes was noted more or less at the same time by Camus, who regarded it as one of the "first signs of the absurd work." See his "Hope and the Absurd in the Work of Franz Kafka," in *The Myth of Sisyphus,* trans. J. O'Brien (New York: Vintage, 1955), p. 93.

5 *La nausée* (Paris: Gallimard, 1938); *Nausea,* trans. Lloyd Alexander (New York: New Directions, n.d.), pp. 29ff. Hereinafter cited *N.*

6 Translated by Tania Stern and James Stern, in *CS* 444; my italics. The resemblance between Roquentin's stone and the philosopher's top has been

pointed out by Maja Goth, *Franz Kafka et les lettres françaises (1928–1955)* (Paris: José Corti, 1956), pp. 142–44.

7   This is a central preoccupation in Kafka. See, for example, "The Problem of Our Laws" (*CS* 437–38) and the letter to Brod of July 1916: ". . . mehr als das, was man sieht, kann ich nicht sagen. Man sieht aber nur allerkleinste Kleinigkeiten. . . . Mehr als Kleinigkeiten kann man mit blossem Auge dort, wo Wahrheit ist, nicht sehn." *Briefe 1902–1924* (Frankfurt am Main: Fischer, 1966), pp. 141–42.

8   Iris Murdoch, *Sartre. Romantic Rationalist* (New Haven: Yale University Press, 1953), p. 13. Murdoch's description of existence as brute, nameless, and escaping our scheme of relations is borrowed from Roquentin's climactic experience with the roots of the chestnut tree (*N* 171, 173, 174). What is rendered as "beastly" in English (*N* 171) is "brute" in the original.

9   Cf. Nietzsche's *Die Geburt der Tragödie*, as quoted in her own English version by Edith Kern, *Existential Thought and Fictional Technique* (New Haven: Yale University Press, 1970), p. 94: "The truth once seen, man now detects everywhere nothing but the ghastly absurdity of existence . . . nausea invades him."

10 Not in the English translation, but see the original: "Übelkeit" and "es wird mir schlecht," in *Der Prozess* (Frankfurt am Main: Fischer, 1971), pp. 53, 54.

11 "Gewohntes Leben," *Der Prozess*, p. 47. The Muirs's "ordinary vocations" (*T* 68) is inaccurate.

12 Trans. Tania Stern and James Stern, in *CS* 33. Cf. Maja Goth, *Franz Kafka*, p. 153.

13 Dominick La Capra, *A Preface to Sartre* (Ithaca: Cornell University Press, 1978), p. 111.

14 Franz Kafka, *Letters to Felice*, ed. Erich Heller and Jürgen Born, trans. James Stern and Elizabeth Duckworth (Harmondsworth: Penguin, 1978), p. 165.

15 Murdoch, *Sartre*, p. 16.

16 Tzvetan Todorov, *Introduction à la littérature fantastique* (Paris: Seuil, 1970), p. 29.

17 See J. E. Cirlot, *A Dictionary of Symbols* (New York: Philosophical Library, 1982), pp. 10–11.

18 See Keith Gore, *Sartre: La Nausée and Les Mouches* (London: Edward Arnold, 1970), p. 22.

19 Maurice Merleau-Ponty, *Sense and Non-Sense* (Evanston, Ill.: Northwestern University Press, 1964), p. 45. Cf. Edith Kern, *Existential Thought and Fictional Technique*, pp. 126–27.

20 Camus thought there was "something rather comic in the lack of proportion between this final hope and the revolt which gave it birth," in *Selected Essays and Notebooks*, ed. Philip Thody (Harmondsworth: Penguin, 1970), p. 169.

21 Sartre, *What Is Literature?*, p. 45.

22 Murdoch, *Sartre*, p. 49.

3 *Sisyphus and Prometheus: Camus and Kafka*

1 "Herman Melville," in Camus, *Selected Essays and Notebooks,* ed. Philip Thody (Harmondsworth: Penguin, 1970), p. 181.

2 Albert Camus, Preface to *Oeuvres Complètes,* by Roger Martin du Gard (Paris: Gallimard, Pléiade Series, 1955), 1:vii.

3 It is appended to *The Myth of Sisyphus,* trans. J. O'Brien (New York: Vintage, 1955), pp. 92–102. Hereinafter cited *MS.* The reference to Kafka's "inspired automata" is on p. 97.

4 See Conor Cruise O'Brien, *Camus* (London: Collins, Fontana Modern Masters Series, 1970), p. 14.

5 This seems to be implied in the following words: "I could see that it makes little difference whether one dies at age of thirty or three-score and ten," from *The Outsider,* trans. Stuart Gilbert (Harmondsworth: Penguin, 1961), p. 112. Hereinafter cited *O.*

6 Sartre, "Camus' *The Outsider,*" in his *Literary and Philosophical Essays,* pp. 36–37.

7 *The Myth of Sisyphus* and *The Outsider* were both published in 1942. The essay on Kafka was appended to the 1948 edition of *The Myth,* but written at the same time as the rest. See Louis Faucon's "Commentaires" to *Le Mythe de Sisyphe,* in Camus's *Essais* (Paris: Gallimard, Pléiade Series, 1965), pp. 1414–16.

8 The distinction between the religious existentialists, who "leap" to God (Kierkegaard, Jaspers) and the atheistic existentialists, who deify history (Husserl, Heidegger, Sartre) is made in the "Interview a 'Servir,'" included in *Essais,* pp. 1427–28.

9 "In Kafka," says Eliseo Vivas, "anguish issues from doubt, in Kierkegaard from certitude." "Kafka's Distorted Mask," in *Kafka. A Collection of Critical Essays,* ed. Ronald Gray (Englewood Cliffs, N.J.: Prentice-Hall, 1962), p. 145.

10 Compare these stone walls (*O* 116) with the "absurd walls" in *The Myth,* p. 8.

11 "Prometheus in the Underworld" (1946), in Camus, *Selected Essays and Notebooks,* p. 131.

12 Sartre, *Literary and Philosophical Essays,* p. 39.

13 Dorrit Cohn, "K. Enters *The Castle.* On the Change of Person in Kafka's Manuscript," *Euphorion* (Heidelberg) 62, no. 1 (1968): 29–30.

14 Shlomith Rimmon, "A Comprehensive Theory of Narrative: Genette's *Figures III* and the Structuralist Study of Fiction," *PTL: A Journal of Descriptive Poetics and Theory of Literature* 1 (1976): 50.

15 D. Cohn, "K. Enters the Castle," pp. 35–36.

16 This casts another doubt on Genette's "neat separation" between "focus" and "voice," which Shlomith Rimmon questions in "A Comprehensive Theory of Narrative," pp. 58–59.

17 Gérard Genette, *Nouveau discours du récit* (Paris: Seuil, 1983), pp. 83–87.

18 John Cruickshank, *Albert Camus and the Literature of Revolt* (New York: Oxford University Press, 1960), p. 152.

19 Genette, *Nouveau discours*, p. 85.

20 Ibid., note 3; my translation.

21 Camus, *The Rebel*, trans. Anthony Bower (New York: Knopf, 1954), pp. 233–34; my italics.

22 Camus, Preface to *Oeuvres Complètes*, by Martin du Gard (see above, note 2), p. vii: "Combiné à l'influence de Kafka . . . ou à la technique americaine du roman de comportement." In an interview given to Jeanine Delpech and published in *Les Nouvelles Littéraires*, November 15, 1945, as quoted by Cruickshank, *Albert Camus*, p. 163, Camus again speaks of the world of the American novel as "a world of automata" and says he "would exchange a hundred Hemingways for a Stendhal or a Benjamin Constant."

23 Kafka, "Reflections on Sin, Pain, Hope, and the True Way," no. 89 in *The Great Wall of China. Stories and Reflections*, trans. Willa Muir and Edwin Muir (New York: Schocken, 1946), p. 302.

4 *The Staircase and Where It Leads:*
Robbe-Grillet and Kafka

1 A. Robbe-Grillet, "From Realism to Reality," in *Snapshots and Towards a New Novel* (London: Calder and Boyars, 1965), p. 156. Hereinafter cited *STNN*.

2 *CS*, pp. 427, 404, 419.

3 See Shimon Sandbank, "Kafka's 'Enigmas': Flight from Pattern," *HSL (Hebrew University Studies in Literature)* 5, no. 2 (1977): 248–64.

4 Prefatory note to *In the Labyrinth*, trans. Christine Brooke-Rose (London: Calder, 1980), p. 5. See Dorrit Cohn, "Castles and Anti-Castles, or Kafka and Robbe-Grillet," *Novel* 5, no. 1 (1971): 29.

5 Quoted by Cohn, ibid., p. 30.

6 Robbe-Grillet, *The Voyeur*, trans. Richard Howard (London: Calder, 1980), pp. 48–49.

7 See pp. 95, 97, 125, 127, and 152 for "yes"; pp. 97, 161, 171, and 182 for "no."

8 See Ann Jefferson, *The Nouveau Roman and the Poetics of Fiction* (Cambridge: Cambridge University Press, 1980), pp. 144–45.

9 Roman Jakobson, "Closing Statement: Linguistics and Poetics," in *Style in Language*, Thomas A. Sebeok (Cambridge, Mass.: MIT Press, 1968), pp. 356, 358.

10 Jefferson, *Nouveau Roman*, p. 168.

11 Robbe-Grillet, *Jealousy*, trans. Richard Howard (London: Calder, n.d.), p. 16.

12 Ibid., pp. 78–79.

13 See Shlomith Rimmon-Kenan, *Narrative Fiction: Contemporary Poetics* (London: Methuen, 1983), pp. 91–94.

14 See Douglas R. Hofstadter, *Gödel, Escher, Bach: an Eternal Golden Braid* (Harmondsworth: Penguin, 1982), p. 10.

15 Robbe-Grillet, *Pour un nouveau roman* (Paris: Minuit, 1963), p. 38.

5 *The Ladder Kicked Away: Beckett and Kafka*

1 Ruby Cohn, *"Watt* in the Light of *The Castle,"* *Comparative Literature* 13 (Spring 1961): 154–66. Beckett is quoted from the *New York Times,* May 6, 1956.

2 Samuel Beckett, *Watt* (London: John Calder, 1963), p. 129. Hereinafter cited *W.*

3 Ruby Cohn, *"Watt,"* p. 162; Raymond Federman, *Journey to Chaos: Samuel Beckett's Early Fiction* (Berkeley: University of California Press, 1965), p. 126; Nathan A. Scott, *Samuel Beckett* (London: Bowes and Bowes, 1969), pp. 51–52; Eugene Webb, *Samuel Beckett: A Study of His Novels* (London: Peter Owen, 1970), p. 17; Edith Kern, "Reflections on the Castle and Mr. Knott's House: Kafka and Beckett," *Proceedings of the Comparative Literature Symposium* 4 (1971): 106–7.

4 Similarly, K. is so tired that he almost misses his first interrogation (*T* 41), is so tired that he wants to get out of the offices (*T* 76–79), goes home "tired, his mind quite blank" after witnessing the whipping (*T* 101), and later on, when deep in guilt, is already exhausted in the morning (*T* 126).

5 See Shimon Sandbank, "Action as Self-Mirror: On Kafka's Plots," *Modern Fiction Studies* 17, no. 1 (1971): 21–29.

6 Interestingly, these first few pages also show some verbal echoes of *The Castle:* the sky is blue over the "secret places," says Arsene (*W* 38), and the Castle's battlements are "clearly outlined against the blue" (*C* 16); the secret places are "indifferent" (*W* 38), and the figure that K. thinks he sees as he looks at the Castle is "untroubled" (*C* 97); the secret places are sites of a being "light and free" (*W* 38), and everything on the Castle hill soars "light and free" (*C* 15); the newcomer at Mr. Knott's house "is come to stay" (*W* 38), and K. tells Frieda "I came here to stay" (*C* 132).

7 Compare *W* 37–38 with *W* 31–36.

8 Federman, *Journey to Chaos,* p. 109.

9 Ibid., p. 128. Cf. Ruby Cohn, *"Watt,"* p. 161.

10 On his first appearance he is either a man, a woman, a parcel, a roll of tarpaulin wrapped up in dark paper and tied with a cord, or a sewer pipe (*W* 14, 16).

11 One is utterly ignorant of his nationality, family, birthplace, confession, occupation, means of existence, distinctive signs (*W* 19); nothing is known about him (*W* 20).

12 "Or was there perhaps some light for Watt, on Mr. Knott, on Watt, in such relations" (*W* 66); "this refusal, by Knott, I beg your pardon, by Watt" (*W* 113).

13 J.-P. Sartre, *Literary and Philosophical Essays* (New York: Collier, 1962), p. 37.

14 In *Proust* (1931; reprint, New York: Grove Press, 1957), p. 71.

15 "Prometheus" and "On Parables," in *CS* 432, 457.

16 See *W* 117–18 and 145–46, and compare Kafka's "Passers-by" (from *Betrachtung*), in *CS* 388.

17 For example, the regression from "Mr. Knott pressed a bell that sounded in Erskine's room" (*W* 118) to "who pressed the bell that sounded in Erskine's

room?" (*W* 120); cf. the withdrawal from "the fight . . . [was] repeated" to "Was it a fight at all?" in *C* 248.

18 For example, "Not that Erskine, Arsene, Walter, Vincent and the others could have told anything of Watt, *except perhaps Arsene a little, and Erskine a little more*, for they could not" (*W* 124; my italics); cf. *Das Schloss* (New York: Schocken, 1946), p. 32: "Es war, wie wenn sich aus dem Summen zahllosen kindlicher Stimmen—*aber auch dieses Summen war keines, sondern nur Gesang fernster, allerfernster Stimmen*—wie wenn sich aus diesem Summen in einer geradezu unmöglichen Weise eine einzige hohe, aber starke Stimme bilde" (my italics). The English (*C* 26) is rather inaccurate in this case.

19 David Shapiro, *Neurotic Styles* (New York: Basic, 1965), pp. 23–53.

20 The phrase is Wilhelm Reich's, in *Character Analysis* (London: Vision, 1973), p. 215.

21 Ibid., pp. 209–10.

22 Quoted from the *New York Times*, May 6, 1956, by Ruby Cohn, "*Watt*," p. 154.

23 See Reich, *Character Analysis*, p. 211.

24 The piece was written in about 1907 and included in *Betrachtung* (1913).

25 See Shimon Sandbank, "Uncertainty as Style: Kafka's *Betrachtung*," *German Life and Letters*, n.s., 24, no. 4 (July 1981): 385–97, especially pp. 387–88.

6 Chairs and Legends: Ionesco and Kafka

1 "The Warden of the Tomb" ("Der Gruftwächter," 1916–17), in *CS* 206–19.

2 Particularly for the Yiddish theatre. See *D*, entry for October 5, 1911, and following.

3 Kafka, *Letters to Friends, Family, and Editors*, trans. R. Winston and C. Winston (London: John Calder, 1978), pp. 114–15.

4 See Stéphane Mosès, "Harav-Mashma'ut Be 'Hagilgul'" (Multiple meaning in *The Metamorphosis*), in *Symposion Kafka* (Tel-Aviv: Sifriyat Po'alim, 1982), pp. 56–59.

5 See Shlomith Rimmon-Kenan, *Narrative Fiction: Contemporary Poetics* (London: Methuen, 1983), p. 76.

6 Eugène Ionesco, *Amédée or How to Get Rid of It* (hereinafter cited *A*), in *Three Plays*, trans. Donald Watson (New York: Grove, 1958), p. 38.

7 See "On the Tram," *CS* 388–89; or the anecdote about the two women in "Description of a Struggle," *CS* 34.

8 "Experience of the Theatre," in Ionesco, *Notes and Counter-Notes*, trans. Donald Watson (London: Calder, 1964), pp. 26–27. Hereinafter cited *NCN*.

9 *The Bald Soprano*, in Ionesco, *Four Plays*, trans. Donald M. Allen (New York: Grove, 1958), p. 22.

10 *The New Tenant*, in *Three Plays*, p. 91. Hereinafter cited *NT*.

11 J. S. Doubrovsky, "Ionesco and the Comic of Absurdity," *Yale French Studies* 23 (Summer 1959): 8–9.

12 A. Robbe-Grillet, "From Realism to Reality," in *Snapshots and Towards a New Novel* (London: Calder and Boyars, 1965), p. 159.

13 Stated in an interview given to Françoise Varenne, "Eugène ouvre ses valises," *Le Figaro*, November 29–30, 1975, p. 24. Compare with Alfred Cismaru, "Ionesco's *L'Homme aux valises:* The Absurdist Turned Classic," *French Review (American Association of Teachers of French)* 50, no. 5 (April 1977): 732–36.

14 Claude Bonnefoy, *Conversations with Eugène Ionesco,* trans. J. Dawson (London: Faber and Faber, 1970), pp. 38–39.

15 Ibid., p. 39. This reading may have been inspired by a reference in Camus's essay "Hope and the Absurd in the Work of Franz Kafka" to "that incalculable amazement man feels at being conscious of the beast he becomes effortlessly." *The Myth of Sisyphus,* trans. J. O'Brien (New York: Vintage, 1955), p. 94.

16 Ibid., pp. 40, 118.

17 In Ionesco, *Four Plays,* p. 110.

18 See above, chapter 3, note 24.

19 Camus, "Hope and the Absurd in the Work of Franz Kafka," pp. 97–98.

20 Calling a doctor is what both Samsa's mother and Berenger, in *Rhinoceros* (Harmondsworth: Penguin, 1962), p. 74 suggest. Elsewhere in *Rhinoceros* it is suggested to consult a solicitor (p. 61), an analyst (p. 95), and the police (p. 82).

21 *Rhinoceros,* pp. 100–101.

22 Ionesco, *Fragments of a Journal,* trans. Jean Stewart (London: Faber and Faber, 1968), p. 27.

23 Ibid., p. 32.

24 Ibid., pp. 33, 72, 119.

25 Ibid., p. 126.

26 Arnold P. Hinchliffe, *The Absurd* (London: Methuen, Critical Idiom Series, no. 5, 1969), p. vii.

27 Ionesco, "Dans les armes de la ville," *Cahiers de la Compagnie Madeleine Renaud-Jean-Louis Barrault* (Paris) 20 (October 1957): 3–5.

28 Compare "In the Long Run I Am for Classicism," *NCN* 135; Bonnefoy, *Conversations with Eugène Ionesco,* p. 127.

29 Bonnefoy, ibid., p. 156.

30 "Le point de depart," *Cahiers des Quatre Saisons,* no. 1 (1955), as translated by Donald Watson in Ionesco, *Plays* (London: John Calder, 1958) 1:viii.

31 Ibid.

32 Ibid.

33 "Hearts Are Not Worn on the Sleeve" is part of Ionesco's London controversy with Kenneth Tynan and included in *NCN*. The quotation is from p. 108.

34 Doubrovsky, "Ionesco and the Comic of Absurdity," p. 6.

35 Compare Kafka's "Excursion into the Mountains": "A pack of nobodies. . . .

How these nobodies jostle each other, all these lifted arms linked together,"
CS 383.

36 Bonnefoy, *Conversations with Eugène Ionesco,* pp. 72–73, 83–85.

37 *The Chairs,* in Ionesco, *Four Plays,* p. 121.

38 Ibid., p. 139.

39 The Old Woman's "ever and ever" echoes the Old Man's "never," ibid., p. 147.

40 "AADIEU ADIEU ARA," ibid., p. 160. In a letter to a producer, Ionesco suggests that the Orator should write just "A A A A A A, nothing but A's," *Notes and Counter-Notes,* p. 198.

41 See chapter 7.

42 Ionesco, *Fragments of a Journal,* p. 46; cf. quotation from Gérard de Nerval, *NCN* 200.

7 *A Sacred Latrine Called Qaphqa: Borges's Kafkaism*

1 J. L. Borges, *The Book of Sand,* trans. N. T. di Giovanni (Harmondsworth: Penguin, 1979), pp. 92–93. Hereinafter cited *BS.*

2 J. L. Borges, *Other Inquisitions 1937–1952,* trans. Ruth L. C. Simms (London: Souvenir, 1973), p. 85. Hereinafter cited *OI.* The contrast between Kafka and Bunyan may well be borrowed from Edwin Muir's introductory note to his translation of *The Castle* (London: Secker, 1930), pp. vii–viii.

3 J. L. Borges, "Las pesadillas y Kafka," *La Prensa* (Buenos Aires) June 2, 1935.

4 J. L. Borges with Margarita Guerrero, *The Book of Imaginary Beings,* trans. N. T. di Giovanni, in collaboration with the author (Harmondsworth: Penguin, 1974), pp. 49, 108. "Crossbreed" is also included in Borges's translation of selected stories by Kafka, *La Metamorfosis,* 5th ed. (1938; reprint, Buenos Aires: Losada, 1965), p. 113.

5 J. L. Borges and A. B. Cesares, *Extraordinary Tales.* ed. and trans. Anthony Kerrigan (London: Souvenir, 1973), pp. 82, 127, 139. Hereinafter cited *ET.* Borges's translations from Kafka also include "Prometheus" and "A Common Confusion," in *La Metamorfosis,* pp. 125, 129.

6 Also in J. L. Borges, *Labyrinths* (Harmondsworth: Penguin, 1970), p. 234. Hereinafter cited *L.*

7 See Stéphane Mosès, "Franz Kafka: 'Das Schweigen der Sirenen,'" in his *Spuren der Schrift: von Goethe bis Celan* (Frankfurt am Main: Jüdischer Verlag bei Athenäum, 1987), pp. 52–72.

8 Borges himself has often used *Don Quixote* as starting point for his own imaginings, as in "Parable of Cervantes and the *Quixote*," "A Problem," and the famous "Pierre Menard, Author of the *Quixote*" (*L* 278, 280, 62). In the latter Borges mentions a "famous plan of Daudet" "to conjoin the Ingenious Gentleman and his squire in *one* figure, which was Tartarin." Kafka also conjoins the two.

9 The unicorn's traditional association with Jesus relates this text to the parable "Paradiso, XXXI, 108" (*L* 274): we have lost the face, we don't know what it was like, any profile in the subway may be Christ's face, it may lurk in every mirror. Compare *D*, entry for August 2, 1917, p. 376: "Usually the one whom you are looking for lives next door. This isn't easy to explain, you must singly accept it as a fact. It is so deeply founded that there is nothing you can do about it, even if you should make an effort to. The reason is that you know nothing of this neighbour you are looking for. That is, you know neither that you are looking for him nor that he lives next door, in which case he very certainly lives next door."

10 This paradox looms large in Borges, notably in his "Avatars of the Tortoise" (*L* 237). It is also quoted in his prologue to *La Metamorfosis*, p. 11. Brecht, in a conversation with Walter Benjamin, also speaks of the analogy between the Achilles and the Tortoise Paradox and Kafka's "The Next Village"; see *Benjamin über Kafka*, ed. Hermann Schweppenhäuser (Frankfurt am Main: Suhrkamp, 1981), p. 153.

11 Borges, *La Metamorfosis*, p. 10: "El motivo de la infinita postergación rige también sus cuentos." Apart from *The Castle*, the following texts by Kafka are then mentioned as illustrating the motif of "infinita postergación": "An Imperial Message" (from "The Great Wall of China"), "The Next Village," "A Common Confusion," and "The Great Wall of China" itself.

12 The same aphorism is quoted in Borge's prologue to *La Metamorfosis*, p. 11.

13 Starting from the "château immense" in the Diderot quotation used as epigraph to the story (*BS* 15; cf. *ET* 68), Oscar Caeiro, in "Borges, por la huella de Kafka," *Criterio* (Buenos Aires), no. 1796 (August 8, 1977):416–21, compares the Congress, which has "something dreamlike about it" (*BS* 19) with the Castle, which is veiled in "mist and darkness" (*C* 9); Ferri's disappointment on seeing Glencoe's ranch and the constructions built for the Congress (*BS* 24–25) with K.'s on seeing the Castle (*C* 15); and the political symbolism of the Congress (democracy) with that of the Castle (feudalism). One could add the scorn, the lowered voices, the alarm or curiosity with which people speak of the Congress (*BS* 18) with similar reactions to the Castle (*C* 16, 20, etc.); and the various races, age groups and physiques represented in the Congress meeting (*BS* 18–19) with the "Nature Theater of Oklahoma" in *America*, trans. E. Muir (New York: New Directions, 1946), pp. 254–55.

14 James E. Irby, Introduction to *Labyrinths*, p. 20.

15 "Bilder, nur Bilder," in Gustav Janouch's *Gespräche mit Kafka* (Frankfurt am Main: S. Fischer, 1951), p. 25.

16 Prologue to *La Metamorfosis*, p. 11.

17 See Leopoldo Azancot, "Borges Y Kafka," *Indice* (Madrid) 17, no. 170 (February 1963): 6.

18 Borges, *A Personal Anthology*, ed. Anthony Kerrigan (New York: Grove, 1967), p. 87. Hereinafter cited *PA*.

19 See Shimon Sandbank, "Action as Self-Mirror: On Kafka's Plots," *Modern Fiction Studies* 17, no. 1 (1971): 21–29.

20 See, for example, "The Aleph," with its obsessive use of the mirror image to express the ineffable experience of the "Aleph" (*PA* 150–53). The idea of the "endlessly repeated images of the double mirror" is related in Borges to the ideas of infinitely smaller units and of infinitely branching paths. See Martin S. Stabb, *Jorge Luis Borges* (New York: Twayne's World Authors, 1970), p. 74.

21 "On Rigor in Science," in Borges, *Dreamtigers*, trans. M. Boyer and H. Morland (London: Souvenir, 1973), p. 90. Hereinafter cited *DT*.

22 Interestingly, however, some of the particulars of this landscape—the infinite (or unfathomable) night, the rose-colored wall—are also part of the mystical experience of "eternidad" Borges describes in "A New Refutation of Time" (*L* 260–62) and repeats in other texts. See Stabb, *Jorge Luis Borges*, p. 69.

23 For other examples from Kafka, notably from the series of aphorisms entitled "He," see Shimon Sandbank, "Structures of Paradox in Kafka," *Modern Language Quarterly* 28, no. 4 (December 1967): 462–72.

24 Prof. Myrna Solotorevsky's unpublished article "The Model of the Midrash in the Work of Borges" (1984) contains helpful comments on the multiversion story.

25 "Prometheus," as mentioned, is one of the texts Borges translated, in *La Metamorfosis*, p. 125.

26 Borges, *In Praise of Darkness*, trans. N. T. di Giovanni (London: Allen Lane, 1975), p. 65. The original is more laconic: "un símbolo de algo que estamos a punto de comprender."

8 *History and the Law: S. Y. Agnon and Kafka*

1 See Arnold J. Band, *Nostalgia and Nightmare. A Study in the Fiction of S. Y. Agnon* (Berkeley and Los Angeles: University of California Press, 1968), p. 187.

2 Y. H. Brenner, "Mehasifrut Veha'itonut Sheba'aretz" (On literature and journalism in Palestine), *Hapo'el Hatsa'ir* (Jerusalem) 2, no. 13 (May 2, 1909).

3 Included, in English translation, in *Twenty-One Stories*, ed. Nahum Glatzer (New York: Schocken, 1961), pp. 65–67. Hereinafter cited *TOS*.

4 *Kol Sipurav shel Sh. Y. Agnon* (The collected stories of S. Y. Agnon), vol. 10: *Samukh Venir'e* (Near and visible) (Jerusalem and Tel-Aviv: Schocken, 1950), pp. 103–249.

5 Gershon Shaked, "He'arot Akhadot Letoldot Hahitkablut shel S. Y. Agnon" (A few notes on the history of Agnon's reception), *Hasifrut*, no. 28 (April 1979): 110.

6 Baruch Kurzweil, "Hakdama Lesefer Hama'asim" (Introduction to the Book of Deeds), in his *Masekhet Haroman* (The web of the novel) (Jerusalem and Tel-Aviv: Schocken, 1953), p. 71. Compare Shaked, "He'arot Akhadot," p. 110, n. 6.

7 Walter Benjamin, "Notizen zu Kafka 'Der Prozess,'" in *Benjamin über Kafka*, p. 114.

8   Ibid., p. 68. Scholem's translation of "Die grosse Synagoge" was published in
    Der Jude 8 (1924): 235–38.
9   Kurzweil, "Hakdama Lesefer," p. 88.
10 Ibid.
11 Robert Alter, *After the Tradition. Essays on Modern Jewish Writing* (New York:
    Dutton, 1969), p. 134.
12 S. Y. Agnon, *Two Tales*, trans. W. Lever (Harmondsworth: Penguin, 1971),
    p. 155.
13 Interestingly, Walter Benjamin in his essay on Kafka likewise applies Kafka's
    way with his parables to his own testament: "The directive in which Kafka
    ordered the destruction of his literary remains is just as unfathomable, to be
    weighed just as carefully as the answers of the doorkeeper before the law," in
    Illuminations, ed. H. Arendt, trans. H. Zohn (New York: Harcourt, Brace and
    World, 1968), p. 124.
14 Agnon, *Samukh Venir'e,* pp. 191–95.
15 Alter, *After the Tradition,* p. 134.
16 See the Talmud reference suggested by Malcom Pasley, "Two Literary Sources
    of Kafka's *Der Prozess,*" *Forum for Modern Language Studies* 3 (1967): 142ff.
17 S. Y. Agnon, *Me'atsmi el Atsmi* (From myself to myself) (Jerusalem and Tel-
    Aviv: Schocken, 1966), p. 245; my translation.
18 Band, *Nostalgia and Nightmare,* p. 448.
19 The verbs "pakar" and "nitpaker," which derive from the same root as "hefker,"
    specifically refer to defection from religion.
20 See chapter 1.
21 Benjamin, *Illuminations,* p. 115.
22 Ibid., p. 128.
23 The distinction is Walter Benjamin's: "Ob sie [die Schrift] den Schülern ab-
    handen gekommen ist oder ob sie sie nicht enträtseln können," letter to Scho-
    lem, August 11, 1934, in *Benjamin über Kafka,* p. 78.
24 See Natan Rotenstreich, "Havayat Hazman Be'Sefer Hama'asim" (The expe-
    rience of time in the Book of Deeds), in *Le' Agnon Shai* (Presented to Agnon),
    ed. Dov Sadan and Ephraim Urbach, 2d ed. (Jerusalem: Jewish Agency Pub-
    lishing House, 1966), pp. 265–79.
25 This reference, as well as several of the following, is borrowed from Gershon
    Shaked, "Galuy Vesamuy Basipur Halo-re'alisti" (The explicit and the implicit
    in the nonrealistic short story), *Hasifrut* 3, no. 2 (November 1971): 260, notes
    19–26.
26 Ibid., p. 265.

9 *Comrade Kafka: Antifascist Fairy Tales of the Thirties*

1   Quoted in J. P. Stern, ed., *The World of Franz Kafka* (London: Weidenfeld and
    Nicolson, 1980), p. 180. The translation is Stern's.

2 See Samuel Hynes, *The Auden Generation. Literature and Politics in England in the 1930s* (London: Bodley Head, 1976), pp. 315–16. Compare Dieter Jakob, "Das Kafka-Bild in England. Zur Aufnahme des Werkes in der journalistischen Kritik 1928–1966," *Oxford German Studies* 5 (1970): 90–143.

3 Joyce Crick, "Kafka and the Muirs," in Stern, *The World of Franz Kafka*, pp. 161–62.

4 Edwin Muir, "Franz Kafka," in his *Essays on Literature and Society* (London: Hogarth, 1949), p. 124.

5 Edward Upward, "Sketch for a Marxist Interpretation of Literature," in *The Mind in Chains. Socialism and the Cultural Revolution*, ed. C. Day Lewis (London: Frederick Muller, 1937), p. 42.

6 Quoted by Jakob, "Das Kafka-Bild in England," p. 120.

7 Edward Upward, *Journey to the Border* (London: Hogarth, 1938), p. 213.

8 See Jakob, "Das Kafka-Bild in England," pp. 115–16; Edwin Muir, *The Present Age from 1914*, vol. 5 of *Introductions to English Literature*, ed. Bonamy Dobrée (London: Cresset, 1939), p. 146.

9 Primarily that of the marquee at the racecourse, a sort of microcosm where the protagonist discovers mankind and himself.

10 Stephen Spender, review of *The Trial* and "The Metamorphosis," in *Life and Letters Today* 17, no. 9 (Autumn 1937): 186.

11 Ibid.

12 Julian Symons, *The Thirties. A Dream Resolved* (London: Cresset, 1960), pp. 152–53; my italics.

13 Muir speaks of Kafka's image of the road in "Franz Kafka" (above, note 4), p. 121. P. H. Butter, *Edwin Muir: Man and Poet* (Edinburgh: Oliver and Boyd, 1966), p. 173, claims that Kafka's use of this image influenced Muir's own poetry subsequent to his work on *The Castle*. For the recurrent figure of the questing hero in English literature in the thirties, see Jakob, "Das Kafka-Bild in England," p. 119.

14 Jiří hájek, "Kafka and the Socialist World" (1967), in *Franz Kafka. An Anthology of Marxist Criticism*, ed. Keneth Hughes (Hanover and London: University of New England, 1981), p. 116.

15 Franz Kafka, *Das Schloss*, 4th ed. (New York: Schocken, 1946), p. 484.

16 Edwin Muir, Introductory note to Kafka's *The Great Wall of China*, trans. Willa Muir and Edwin Muir (New York: Schocken, 1946), pp. xiv–xv.

17 Ruthven Todd, *Over the Mountain* (London: Falcon, 1946), p. 17. Hereinafter cited *OM*.

18 Rex Warner, *The Wild Goose Chase* (London: John Lane, Bodley Head, 1945), pp. 79–80. Hereinafter cited *WGC*.

19 Rex Warner, *The Aerodrome* (Harmondsworth: Penguin, 1945), pp. 9–10, 101. Hereinafter cited *A*.

20 Ruthven Todd, *The Lost Traveller* (New York: Dover, 1968), p. 47. Hereinafter cited *LT*.

21 Kafka, *Das Schloss,* p. 488.

22 Ibid.

23 Erich Heller, "The World of Franz Kafka," in his *The Disinherited Mind* (Harmondsworth: Penguin, 1961), pp. 196–97.

24 Rex Warner, "The Allegorical Method," in his *The Cult of Power. Essays* (London: John Lane, Bodley Head, 1946), pp. 109–10. The distinction is borrowed from Muir's introductory note to his translation of *The Castle* (London: Secker, 1930), p. ix.

25 H. A. Mason, "The English Kafka," *Scrutiny* 14, no. 2 (December 1946): 156–58 (a review of R. Warner's *The Cult of Power*).

26 Warner, "The Allegorical Method," p. 111.

27 D. J. Enright, "The Use and Misuse of Symbolism," in *Focus One,* ed. Balachandra Rajan and H. Pearse (London: D. Dobson, 1945), p. 38. Compare John Atkins, "On Rex Warner," ibid., pp. 33–37; Louis Adeane, "The Hero Myth in Kafka's Writing," ibid., p. 56; George Woodcock, "Kafka and Rex Warner," ibid., p. 60; Peter Demetz, "Kafka in England," *German Life and Letters,* n.s., 4 (1950): 24; A. A. De Vitis, "Rex Warner and the Cult of Power," in *The Achievement of Rex Warner,* ed. A. L. McLeod (Sydney: Wentworth, 1965), pp. 50–51.

28 For example, *A* 85, 111, 114, 126, and compare *T* 132–33: "any particular case thus appeared in their circle of jurisdiction often without their knowing whence it came, and passed from it they knew not whither." It is significant, of course, that Roy later learns of the overall purpose of the organization, while K. learns nothing.

29 By Demetz, "Kafka in England," p. 30.

30 This is Sartre's requirement from the fantastic: see chapter 2.

31 See Shimon Sandbank, "Action as Self-Mirror: On Kafka's Plots," *Modern Fiction Studies* 17, no. 1 (1971): 21–29.

10 Hina *and* Hoti: *Kafka and American Fiction*

1 John Barth, *The End of the Road* (Harmondsworth: Penguin, 1967), p. 80, hereinafter cited *ER*; Thomas Pynchon, *V.* (New York: Bantam, 1964), p. 259.

2 It is also early in Barth's career, and very different from his later work, to which my conclusions need not apply.

3 See chapter 1.

4 Most conspicuously in "Life-Story," in *Lost in the Funhouse* (New York: Bantam, 1981), pp. 113–26.

5 I owe this point to Mrs. Shlomit Ilan.

6 It murders the officer as he tries to make it inscribe the new liberal concept of justice on his body: see *CS* 161–66.

7 Kurt Vonnegut, *Cat's Cradle* (New York: Dell, 1981), p. 118. Hereinafter cited *CC*.

8 Paul de Man, "The Rhetoric of Temporality," in *Interpretation: Theory and Practice,* ed. C. H. Singleton (Baltimore: Johns Hopkins University Press, 1969), p. 174.

9 Cf. Tony Tanner, *City of Words. American Fiction 1950–1970* (London: J. Cape, 1971) p. 174.

10 Thomas Pynchon, *The Crying of Lot 49* (New York: Bantam, 1967), pp. 134–35.

11 Frank Kermode, *The Genesis of Secrecy* (Cambridge: Harvard University Press, 1979), p. 33.